HOW TO RECOGNIZE & REWARD EMPLOYEES

SECOND EDITION

HOW TO RECOGNIZE & REWARD EMPLOYEES

150 Ways to Inspire Peak Performance

SECOND EDITION

Donna Deeprose

AMERICAN MANAGEMENT ASSOCIATION

New York • Atlanta • Brussels • Chicago • Mexico City • San Francisco
Shanghai • Tokyo • Toronto • Washington, D.C.

This publication is designed to provide accurate and authoritative
information in regard to the subject matter covered. It is sold with the
understanding that the publisher is not engaged in rendering legal,
accounting, or other professional service. If legal advice or other expert
assistance is required, the services of a competent professional person
should be sought.

Library of Congress Cataloging-in-Publication Data

Deeprose, Donna.
  How to recognize & reward employees : 150 ways to inspire peak performance /
Donna Deeprose.— 2nd ed.
   p. cm. — (WorkSmart series)
  Includes index.
  ISBN-10: 0-8144-7331-8 (pbk.)
  ISBN-13: 978-0-8144-7331-3 (pbk.)
  1. Incentives in industry. 2. Employee motivation. I. Title: How to
recognize and reward employees. II. Title. III. Series.

 HF5549.5.I5D43 2006
 658.3'142—dc22

                   2006007482

Printing number

10 9 8 7 6 5 4 3 2

CONTENTS

———————

PART THREE

150 WAYS TO RECOGNIZE AND REWARD EMPLOYEES

PREFACE

The first edition of this book came out twelve years ago. The economy was inching out of a recession that had cost profits and jobs and cracked the façade of employer-employee loyalty that had marked decades of corporate expansion. Companies were pared close to the bone in terms of personnel, and although it was a time of cautious optimism, salary increase budgets were still low and likely to remain that way. So a book on recognizing and rewarding employees that focused more on treating people well than on giving them big raises made a lot of sense.

A lot has happened in the intervening twelve years. First, there were years of economic expansion, riding on the technology wave. There were plenty of tales of ordinary people in low-level jobs becoming instant millionaires when start-up dot.coms floated their initial public offerings. That scenario changed recognition and reward expectations even in traditional companies. Jobs were still insecure, but bonuses became more common, and many people began to wonder if they wouldn't do better in business for themselves anyway.

Then the dot-com bubble burst, as venture capital dried up when the economy took a nosedive in 2001. Suddenly, there were dot-com wunderkinds out looking for jobs alongside the long-displaced factory workers. A series of high-profile executive scandals shook the corporate world, tainting the reputations not just of individual companies but also of entire industries and undermining the public's confidence in big business as a whole.

Expectations for rewards changed again, but perhaps not as much as one might think. Indeed, surveys showed that job security moved upward on the list of things workers valued most, but these newly displaced workers were the famous Gen Xers. Their attitudes toward work varied greatly from those of their baby boomer parents, whose single-minded climb up the corporate ladder had been chronicled repeatedly. The Gen Xers' credo was work smarter, not harder. They demanded exciting challenges, immediate recognition, and plenty of time for a full life outside of their jobs. And a few years of hard times didn't entirely wipe out those expectations.

In a way, this new edition comes at a time that parallels the timeframe of the original edition. The economy is expanding again, and people are cautiously optimistic once more. Even dot-coms are flourishing, although not in the frenzied, anything-goes mode of the late 1990s. Companies are expecting to grow their revenues and profits again—but not necessarily their workforces. With that goal in mind, they are looking for ways to reduce turnover because it is costly and leaves skill holes that are difficult to fill. And they are constantly looking for ways to increase productivity through ever-improving performance.

However, achieving these objectives requires companies to confront new issues:

- **Company loyalty, which was only cracked in 1994, is shattered now.** Through two decades of downsizings, older workers have learned bitterly to rely on their own skills and marketability, not on any expectations that faithful service will be rewarded by lifetime employment. And younger workers, having had no experience with the old form of job security, take job-hopping as the norm.

- **In the wake of headline-making scandals, companies have to prove their integrity to earn employees' pride in working for them.** In the past, companies rushed to codify sets of values, ostensibly to remind themselves constantly of what they stood for, instill pride in their employees, and impress their customers. But publishing the right words isn't enough anymore. The most admired companies prove they live their values by their actions and by what they reward employees for doing.

■ **The work/life balance has emerged as a defining societal issue of the new century.** The two-income family changed the norm. First, female workers demanded conditions that allowed them to meet family obligations as well as to have meaningful careers. As men began to share those obligations toward home and family, they too looked for alternatives to their traditional role of breadwinner first, family member second. And the Gen Xers started out with expectations of lives that encompassed much more than long hours at work. Leading companies realized that recruiting and retaining the best workers required designing a whole new work environment.

In response to twelve years of change, this edition of *How to Recognize & Reward Employees* is focused somewhat differently from the original. Part I of both editions starts with Three Reasons to Recognize and Reward Employees. However, in the original edition, these reasons reflected employees' needs: equity, motivation, and clarification. This edition starts with the organization's needs: grow income and profits, retain crucial employees, and inspire peak performance. The good news is that the responses to these needs are very much the same in both books. The best companies have learned that their needs and those of their employees can be met through many of the same actions.

Part II of the book still contains Ten Guidelines for Recognizing and Rewarding Employees, but the guidelines have been remolded to include the new emphasis on values and a work/life balance. Finally, Part III grew from 100 Ways to Recognize and Reward People to 150 Ways, as effective organizations have become more resourceful and ingenious in how they reward employees by demonstrating many new examples.

ACKNOWLEDGMENTS

I started this new edition with a plea for help from a group of people who have shared their considerable knowledge and experience with me for many years. Some of them are referenced in the text for the specific recognition and reward suggestions they offered. Others, like Florence Stone, Bill Becker, and Vicki Axelrod broadened my perspective as I planned this new edition. And, as so often before, Roz Gold set me back me on target when I bogged down. My thanks to all of them and to the people who described the outstanding recognition and reward programs in the companies referenced in the book.

1

THREE REASONS TO RECOGNIZE AND REWARD EMPLOYEES

The most important reason to recognize and reward employees is that it makes good business sense. Doing so effectively helps organizations to do the following:

- Grow their revenues and profits
- Retain their best employees and recruit top new talent
- Inspire peak performance from all their employees

GROW YOUR REVENUE AND PROFITS

I t makes sense intuitively that recognizing and rewarding employees for their superior performance leads to superior organizational performance. Most employers will tell you that optimal performance is what they expect to achieve with their rewards programs.

However, when times are tough, it is not intuition that drives policy in most companies but rather bottom-line results. So, if you need a good reason to invest more creative effort and money in your rewards program or to convince your company to do so, you should forget intuition and look for evidence of hard numbers.

> Recognizing and rewarding employees does more than make people happy. Solid numbers show that it contributes directly to bottom-line results.

Let's take a look at the results achieved at Medtronic, Inc., of Minneapolis, Minnesota, a leading global producer of medical technology. Medtronic has a unique way of encouraging its employees' out-of-the box creativity. Through its Quest program, the company rewards qualified employees with seed money in the amounts of $5,000 to $50,000 to pursue innovative ideas outside their normal responsibilities. Although employees are expected to keep up with their normal responsibilities, Quest grant winners are allowed to spend at least 10 percent of their time for a year pursuing their own projects. Some projects take less time; a few take more. At any given time, Medtronic may have ongoing approximately twenty-five Quest projects throughout the company.

Quest grant winners get recognition, challenging new work, and the resources to bring their ideas to life. Medtronic has received a range of new technology to expand its product line: a new pacemaker system, the world's first implantable cardiac monitor, and a therapeutic gel made from blood platelets for use on hard-to-heal wounds—to name just a few.

Over the past several years, work/life programs that benefit the entire workforce have risen high on employees' list of most-valued rewards. Goldman Sachs, the New York City–based global investment banking firm, is one of many companies that offers its employees subsidized child care. Goldman Sachs sweetens that program with up to forty days of free backup care at on-site and off-site locations, plus an additional twenty days for parents of infants making the transition back to work. What's in it for the company? Its records show that employees who use child care have a 2.6 percent lower voluntary termination rate than eligible nonusers. In 2004, the company calculated that the backup program forestalled 57,490 hours of absence by parents who would otherwise have had to take time off to stay with their children when bad weather closed schools, regular babysitters called in sick, or other emergencies arose. That translated into about $5 million in savings.

The measurable results from these companies are powerful evidence that effective rewards programs have significant bottom-line impact. However, the collected proof is even broader.

The Jackson Organization, a research firm in Columbia, Maryland, surveyed twenty-six thousand employees in twenty-six companies to measures the connection between employee recognition and profitability. It published the results in 2005 in a study called "Employee Recognition and Profitability: Making the Connection." The study correlates responses to the statement "My organization recognizes excellence" to three measures of profitability: return on equity (ROE), return on assets

(ROA), and operating margin. Organizations whose employees feel they are recognized for excellent performance outperform companies whose employees do not on all three counts: by more than 3:1 on ROE and ROA and by a resounding 6:1 on Operating Margin.

> Companies like Medtronic, Goldman Sachs, and Carlson Companies, whose reward programs tie directly to company business results, have earned places on Fortune's 100 Best Companies to Work For list in recent years.

To reinforce the connection between rewards and business results, some companies focus their rewards programs directly on their strategies for success. Carlson Companies, a leader in the marketing, travel, and hospitality industries, has a program called Bravo that allows employees to recognize each other. Anyone—manager or employee—can recognize another individual or team for actions aligned with company strategies such as Build the Team, Satisfy the Customer, Deliver Our Family of Businesses, or Work Smarter, Not Harder.

For example, if you worked for a Carlson business unit, such as Carlson Marketing Worldwide, and you wanted to thank a colleague in another Carlson business unit—such as Carlson Hotels Worldwide—for help in a cross-business project, it would fall under the strategy Deliver Our Family of Businesses. You would go online to CarlsonRewards, Carlson's recognition website, and fill out a Bravo recognition form, where you'd select that strategy and describe the person's contribution. Nominees get certificates signed by the heads of their business units. They are also eligible to receive Gold Points (through the accumulation of Bravos or sweepstakes drawings). These Gold Points are redeemable for merchandise and gift certificates. An employee who collected enough Bravo points could even redeem them for a cruise, but most employees redeem theirs more frequently, selecting prizes like Target gift cards or small merchandise items.

Bravo recipients get recognition from peers and top executives and are also able to receive rewards of their choice. Carlson wins because the program encourages behavior that supports company strategy for building the business and building better relationships.

Five Questions to Ask Yourself

Check the box if the statement is true for you:

❑   My organization recognizes its employees for excellent performance.

❑   My organization measures the impact of its rewards programs.

❑   Our rewards programs are directly aligned with company strategy.

❑   When I get rewarded, I know what that reward is for and how my actions contributed to organizational strategy.

❑   When I reward people who work for me, they know what the reward is for and how their actions contributed to organizational strategy.

THE ROLE OF MANAGERS IN RECOGNIZING AND REWARDING EMPLOYEES

This chapter has presented examples of company-wide recognition and rewards programs that support company growth. However, first-line and even middle managers often have little or no say in developing or implementing these programs and express frustration over the limits of their ability to influence the rewards their employees receive. If that describes you, take this brief true/false quiz to examine your own expectations of the managers' role in recognizing and rewarding employees:

1. If the people who report to me feel they are not being fairly rewarded, there is nothing I can do about it. It's the fault of the organization's compensation system.   T   F

2. The only way to get employees to do more or better work is to pay them more.   T   F

3. When times are tough, just having a job is reward enough for many employees.   T   F

4. Some of the people who report to me have a very inflated idea of their

own worth. They expect above-average rewards for pretty mediocre
performance.   T   F

5. What other employees make is no business of anyone who reports to
me and people have no right to compare their salaries to anyone else's.   T   F

6. I'm tired of hearing that other companies pay better than this one. If my
employees think some other company is so great, let them get jobs
there.   T   F

7. The best way to make pay equitable among the people who work for
me is to pay them all about the same.   T   F

8. If people who report to me complain that employees in other parts of
the company earn more than they do, I point out that I'm in the same
boat, making less than many other managers, too.   T   F

9. If I can't give an employee the raise I think the person deserves, I
promise to make it up next year.   T   F

10. The happiest employees are those who make the most money.   T   F

SCORING

If you answered "true" to any of the questions in the preceding quiz, the goal of this book is to change your mind and to provide you with new ideas and techniques for dealing with the problems involved. You'll find most of the issues covered in more depth in succeeding chapters, but here is a quick analysis:

1. **False.** Through the manner in which they communicate and apply the compensation system, managers can influence employees' perception of the system's fairness. Equally important is to recognize that salary is only one of several components that make up an organization's total rewards package. Managers can create an environment that boosts employees' self-esteem, provides opportunities for creativity and growth, and allows employees to enjoy the rewards that are inherent in interesting and challenging work.

2. **False.** Actually, increased pay quickly becomes an entitlement rather than an incentive to work more productively. Recogni-

tion and the intrinsic rewards noted in the analysis of question 1 are often more effective in the long run.

3. **False.** Just having a job may be reward enough to keep people coming to work in tough times, but fear of losing it tends to encourage employees to retract into safe, conventional behavior and avoid the innovation and risk taking that leads to break-through organizational performance.

4. **False.** Managers should ensure that their employees know, for each of their tasks, what represents unsatisfactory, average, and above-average performance and what kind of compensation they can expect for each level.

5. **False.** Whether employees should know what other people earn is irrelevant. They do find out. Managers who ignore employee resentment about perceived inequities should expect that resentment to build and to affect performance.

6. **False.** Managers with that attitude lose their best workers and retain only those not good enough to get better paying jobs elsewhere. On the other hand, good workers will often stay with an organization that pays less than its competitors pay if the total reward package (see the analysis of question 1) is favorable and distributed fairly within the organization.

7. **False.** Paying everyone the same wage encourages mediocre performance from everyone and builds resentment among the best performers.

8. **False.** Sharing your own salary dissatisfactions with your employees undermines your credibility and their sense of satisfaction in working for you. Rather than sanctioning their dissatisfaction, focus on building a work environment that makes working for your unit its own reward.

9. **False.** Despite your best intentions, too much can happen in a year to undermine your ability to fulfill your promise. If you don't, the affected employee will become doubly embittered.

10. **False.** The happiest and most productive employees are those who enjoy doing their work and who are recognized for their accomplishments.

RETAIN YOUR BEST EMPLOYEES AND RECRUIT TOP NEW TALENT

here is a paradox confronting most organizations today of how to maintain a lean workforce by downsizing when costs rises and/or sales decline, while at the same time retain key employees and crucial skills without any promise of long-term job security. Not that most workers expect that kind of security now, but without it what is to keep them from jumping ship first, from moving on at the first prospect of a few more dollars or a new work challenge?

In fact, most companies rate retaining and recruiting as their number one personnel issue. The question is: What do you give talented workers to make them want to join your organization and stay there as long as you have work for them to do?

A FAIR DAY'S WORK FOR A FAIR DAY'S . . . WHAT?

All organizations acknowledge the need to establish an equitable balance between each employee's contribution to the organization and that of the organization to the employee. Meeting that need is basic to recruiting and retaining talent. However, exactly what reward balances a proverbial fair day's work?

A fair day's pay? Certainly, that is the first thing that comes to mind. Nevertheless, many managers feel they have little control over the paychecks of the people who work for them. Locked into an organization-wide compensation system, managers are often frustrated by the narrow latitude they have for adjusting wages and salaries to fit each employee's hopes and expectations. However, even first-line managers have a significant role to play in balancing work and pay. We will explore this role later in this chapter.

Nevertheless, the realization that pay is not the only thing people work for is equally important. Employees are looking for a number of other returns to justify the time, energy, and mental and emotional effort they devote to the organization. That is why many organizations now think in terms of a total rewards package. This type of package includes not just salary and benefits but also work environment, learning and development, and work/life balance. Equity requires that total rewards meet the needs of employees to the same degree that employees contribute to meeting the objectives of the organization.

THREE EQUITY EQUATIONS

This balance can be summed up in Equity Equation 1:

> *What the employee receives from the employer must be equal in value to the quality and quantity of work done by the employee.*

For employees to verify Equity Equation 1, they must have a way to determine the worth of their work. To some degree they do this by gut feel, but they validate their feelings by making two comparisons. They compare what they receive from their employer to what other people in the organization receive for doing similar work. And they compare what they receive to what is received by people doing similar work in other organizations. These comparisons give rise to two more equity equations.

According to Equity Equation 2:

What the employee receives from the employer must be equal in value to what is received by other employees doing similar work of similar quality and quantity.

Equity Equation 3 is:

What the employee receives from the employer must be equal in value to what is received by people who do similar work for other organizations.

In recent years, the equity equations have gained another component—and for some people it is a troublesome one. Many workers are questioning the equity of their rewards compared with those of top management, whose rewards are frequently exponentially higher. With so many revelations of top executives earning almost unfathomable amounts of money while leading organizations into financial disaster, the disparity between even middle rungs on the ladder and the top ones can contribute to festering dissatisfaction.

In making equity comparisons, the first thing employees weigh is paychecks, but as they balance the equations for themselves they will factor in other things, such as opportunities to do interesting and challenging work, the recognition they receive for their accomplishments, or even the ambience of their working environment. A single work unit or an entire company in which the total rewards are clearly superior can keep loyal, high-performing employees even if the financial rewards are lower than in other units or other organizations.

STAND OUT FROM THE CROWD

In fact, in the competition to recruit and retain top talent, an organization can best differentiate itself as an employer of choice through the nonfinancial components of its total rewards package. Companies that stand out provide a unique work experience by offering rewards that not only meet their employees' needs but also affirm strong values that make workers proud.

It's not the money, but unique, value-based rewards that differentiate employers of choice.

The Timberland Company of Stratham, New Hampshire, a regular on both the *Fortune* and the *Working Mother* lists of Best Companies to Work For, offers rewards of that kind. Timberland, which manufactures outdoor footwear, apparel, and accessories, defines itself on its website by its efforts to be "a twenty-first century example for socially responsible corporations around the world." The company invests in social and environmental programs both close to home and abroad, and it encourages employees to become personally involved in community service and environmental stewardship through its Path of Service™ and Service Sabbatical programs. Timberland's Path of Service™ program is an employee benefit granting up to forty paid hours per year to participate in volunteer activities. Employees who have been with Timberland for at least one year can apply for a paid Service Sabbatical to devote themselves to volunteer full-time at a nonprofit of their choice for up to six months.

Fabienne Hooper, a process integrity manager at Timberland, takes advantage of her forty hours every year to volunteer with community projects. During her eleven years with the company, she has joined coworkers to adopt a piece of a highway, volunteered at the local YMCA where she was on the board of advisors, and even gone to an environmental camp. When her kids were little, she saved one day a year for each, to chaperone a school field trip. It was a great way, she says, for a single mom to stay involved with her children's activities.

When Timberland began offering sabbaticals, she fantasized about applying to work in the Third World somewhere for six months, but the project she became truly passionate about was right at home. Her youngest son was having trouble at school and she began looking for an alternative school that would stimulate him academically. The school that grabbed her interest, Cocheco Arts and Technology Academy in Dover, New Hampshire, hadn't yet opened. Characteristically, she pitched in as a volunteer to get it going and was elected to the board of trustees. Scheduled to open in January 2005, the school had an opening for an administrative position but couldn't afford to pay a salary.

Hooper's reaction was "What a great opportunity for me." With a six-month sabbatical, she was able to help the academy get off the ground and be in her son's school at the same time.

"Just think of it," she enthused, "you get six months leave from your job to do something else—and you get paid for it."

Hooper doesn't have to be asked what all this means in terms of loyalty. "Before I came to Timberland, I never worked anywhere for more than three years," she said. "Now there is no reason to go anywhere else." And, incidentally, her son is doing just fine at his new school.

WAYS TO BE SPECIAL ON A SHOESTRING

If your company is very small or you are managing a single unit, big-ticket programs like those of Timberland are probably out of your reach. However, these high-profile perks are not always necessary to make you the preferred employer among organizations comparable to yours.

According to Patti Dowse, president of Erda Leather, which makes leather and fabric handbags in Cambridge, Maine, "This is an ongoing problem for a small business, trying to retain quality people. In order to be competitive in a global market, prices need to stay low, and with them the budget for compensation. So we have to be rewarding in other ways."

Dowse offers perks that are particularly appropriate to her business and her employees, such as the following:

- A massage therapist who comes to the company to do chair massages, which are a welcome treat to workers who spend their days bent over sewing machines or cutting boards

- A Christmas party at which workers help each other make gifts using Erda materials and machines

- Keeping the facility open for employees to use on their own time to make whatever they wish

- Flextime, allowing employees to choose whatever hours work best for them and their families

- Trips with Dowse to New York or Philadelphia for trade shows

But perhaps the most rewarding benefit is the kind of environment Dowse strives to create at Erda. "I find that what people want most in their work life is a sense of ownership and control," she explained.

Therefore, she consults with everyone on matters not customarily brought up to employees. When business blossomed into more than they could comfortably handle, she got their input into how much they could raise prices. She has also asked their opinions on fabric choices, advertising images, and new styles. "Is this fabric hard to sew? To cut? Does this style take too long to sew?"

Cross training helps employees to learn new jobs and brings fresh insights about each task. "Keeping folks stimulated is always a challenge in repetitive work," Dowse admitted.

Every employee is quality control. If just one person thinks a piece should be a second, then it is. It is a way to let people know their opinions are respected and that the company takes the same pride they do in quality work.

BUT WHAT ABOUT MONEY?

Certainly money is the most obvious component in the equity equations, so its importance as a reward cannot be dismissed—nor can its power to lure good workers over to your competitors. Here is another paradox: In surveys of information technology (IT) workers in particular, respondents said what they wanted most were things like job challenge, flexible schedules, and additional time off. But more money was right up at the top of the list of reasons for changing jobs.[1]

> The best-performing companies do not always pay the highest salaries, but they do pay their top performers much better than their average ones.

Despite the lure of greener money on the other side of the fence, it is not the size of the salary budget that differentiates between companies that retain their key workers and those that lose them, but rather the way raises are distributed. The greater the differentiation between the financial rewards paid to top and poor performers, the better the retention record.

Managers can influence how employees perceive the equity of their income and their raises by rewarding above-average performance evaluations with above-average pay increases. The perception of equity breaks down when employees rated "excellent" or "exceptional" receive only average pay raises. This is a problem in work units where all or most of the employees are highly regarded workers who have regularly been rated very highly. Without some poor performers to balance the high ones, managers find it difficult to give above-average raises to everyone and stay within their budgets. Some managers appeal successfully to upper management for a bigger share of the pie. Otherwise, it may be time to rethink the meaning of average. Logically, if everyone is performing above average, the perception of average is too low. Some managers may need to raise the bar at the beginning of a performance cycle and let employees know early on that they need to meet specific challenges to earn a higher rating and a higher raise.

If you are afraid to differentiate sharply between star performers and average ones for fear of losing steady, reliable people you depend on for doing a large share of your unit's work, there are other ways of keeping these people. They'll respond favorably to well-thought-out nonmonetary rewards and to a positive work environment with opportunities to increase their skills, nonmonetary recognition for the support they provide the unit, flexible work schedules, and adaptation by the company to their work/life needs.

A Checklist for Applying the Principles of Equity

In the perception of those who report to you, which equity equations need balancing in your work unit? Check all that apply.

❏   Reward equals work.

❏   Employees receive comparable rewards for comparable work.

❏   Rewards in the organization are comparable with rewards in other organizations.

What can you do to begin to balance the equity equations in the perception of your employees? Check all that apply.

- ❏ At the beginning of the salary year, or the start of the performance management cycle, ensure that each employee knows, for each part of the job, what represents unsatisfactory, average, and above-average performance.

- ❏ With employee input, redefine average and above-average performance to ensure that truly above-average performers earn above average-salary increases.

- ❏ Focus on meeting employee needs for creative challenge, professional growth, and work/life balance.

- ❏ Begin to build a work environment that makes working in your unit its own reward.

NOTE

1. *InformationWeek Research National Salary Survey of 12,158 IT Professionals*, Spring 2005, and Foote Partners *2005 IT Retention Study*.

INSPIRE PEAK PERFORMANCE

D uring the course of two stays at Ibis Hotels in Portugal, one feature stood out. The performance of employees staffing the reception desks at this moderately priced chain was outstanding. They were warm, welcoming, and helpful beyond the typical behavior of their counterparts in most luxury hotels. What's more, they always gave the impression of enjoying their jobs.

"What does Ibis do to reward you for treating customers this way?" I asked Humberto Reis at the Évora Ibis, after he had eased me through a late-night tourist crisis. His usual smile broadened further. "Accor Group [Ibis' parent company] puts employees first," he said. "It is very imaginative in how it rewards employees."

Reis said he had received bonuses for learning additional languages (his English was excellent), suggestions for improvements that had been implemented by the hotel, selling Accor cards (subscription cards for frequent guests), and for participating in specific challenges, such as promoting and improving the restaurant. In addition, he said, most higher level positions are filled through promotions from within.

Many corporate managers dream of having employees as motivated as Reis and his fellow reception desk staffers.

CAN YOU MOTIVATE ANOTHER PERSON?

Purists insist that no one can motivate another person, that all motivation comes from within. Therefore, the best way to start this chapter is with a definition of terms. What this book means by *motivating* other people is inspiring individuals and teams to do the best possible job by creating an environment in which they want to perform to the best of their abilities. That definition recognizes that there are plenty of ways a manager can influence the strength of an employee's internal motivation.

One thing a manager can do is to provide incentives, in the form of recognition and rewards, to encourage people to maintain excellent performance and to improve unsatisfactory performance. Invariably the first incentive that comes to mind is money, but for most managers, motivating with money confronts two obstacles. The first is their limited control over financial awards for their employees. The second is that money's success as a motivator is inconsistent.

IS MONEY A MOTIVATOR?

That's a very old question with no easy answer. Greek playwright Sophocles wrote in *Antigone*, "There is nothing in the world so demoralizing as money." Euripides said in *Medea*, "Money is far more persuasive than logical arguments."

You'd think people would have figured it out by now. Some current credible studies conclude that yes, money is a motivator. But equally credible studies conclude that no, it is not. And both studies are right—it is and it isn't—depending upon how you use money. Here is what top-performing companies have found:

- **Salaries are not motivators.** They are entitlements. Certainly, salaries are a primary reason people hold jobs, but they are not the primary reason people do superior work. An exceptional raise might drive a brief spurt of energized behavior, but ardor diminishes as living expenses swell to meet the raise (as they always do). Of course, the dark side of entitlements is that diminishing them is very demotivating, so withholding a raise from someone who has every reason to expect one can have a very negative affect on that person's motivation.

■ **The expectation of a financial reward is motivating.** This is especially true when the recipient knows exactly what to do to get it. Promises of bonuses based on clear criteria encourage people to meet those criteria. It is motivating to know that when you learn a language, you'll get a bonus, as Reis did at Ibis. It is motivating to know that if you achieve goals you set at the beginning of the year, you'll get an incentive bonus at year-end, especially if you and your manager meet regularly to discuss your progress throughout the year, so that you know exactly where you stand and what more you have to do at all times.

■ **Occasional spot bonuses are motivating.** They don't even have to be big; especially for workers in lower-paid industries, $50 to $100 is effective. Small bonuses work when they are presented for specific behaviors or achievements, immediately after the noteworthy performance. A spot bonus is really an exceptionally nice thank-you. It makes the recipient feel special and appreciated. Paradoxically, there is some evidence that frequent spot bonuses are not particularly motivating. They fall into the entitlement sphere.

As a motivator, money has another characteristic that has to be taken into account: It acts as a scorecard. It is one way people measure their achievement, their importance to the organization, and their standing among others in the organization as well as in their community.

"Money is how you keep score."
    —Many people have said it, but the first was probably H. Wayne Huizenga, billionaire entrepreneur (quoted in *The New York Times Magazine,* December 5, 1993).

But money needn't be the only way to keep score. Managers with little access to financial rewards for their employees can give points to their workers in a variety of other, often more motivating ways. Many people are motivated by things that money cannot measure at all.

IF NOT MONEY, THEN WHAT?

People are motivated to fulfill a number of different needs, the most basic being the need to get a roof over their heads and food in their mouths. The most lofty need perhaps is to transcend the mundane and reach the highest level of achievement and spirituality (what motivation theorist Abraham Maslow called *self-actualization*). However, what drives people the strongest varies from one individual to another and for any individual may change depending on the situation. At any given time, an individual may be driven primarily by the need for security, socialization, esteem, achievement, or power—or some combination of these factors.

The reward that an employee values most—and that provides the greatest incentive to maintain and improve performance—will be one that contributes to the fulfillment of that person's strongest drives. The challenge for the manager is to recognize what each employee is seeking and to identify ways to reward the employee by satisfying that need.

EXERCISE 1

NONMONETARY REWARDS THAT MOTIVATE

The columns in the worksheet below contain: first, descriptions of employees; second, a list of possible driving needs; and third, a list of various rewards. For each employee, determine the most likely driving need and the two rewards that are most appropriate for fulfilling that need. (Use a reward only once even though some rewards may seem appropriate for fulfilling more than one need. Try to select the best two for each need.)

Employees	**Needs**	**Rewards**

I. The employee has complained about feeling isolated and needing more interaction with others on the job.

Probable need:

_____

Appropriate rewards:

_____

_____

II. A good worker who is helpful to others, the employee writes you memos documenting each of her accomplishments.

Probable need:

_____

Appropriate rewards:

_____

_____

III. The employee constantly seeks new assignments and dedicates himself to solving problems and mastering challenges.

Probable need:

_____

Appropriate rewards:

_____

_____

IV. Although the employee's job is not in serious danger, she has become nervous and withdrawn as the company has gone through a series of downsizings.

Probable need:

_____

Needs

(a) security
(b) socializing
(c) esteem
(d) achievement
(e) power

Rewards

1. A letter to your boss praising the worker and a copy of it given to the employee
2. The right to choose and manage a project
3. A department party
4. An opportunity to work on a project team
5. An opportunity to learn new skills that are greatly in demand in the organization
6. An opportunity to help develop an important new product for the company
7. Testimonials from peers, attesting to their high regard for the employee
8. A team leadership assignment
9. Assurances that the employee's job is not in danger of being eliminated
10. An assignment to develop and implement a program that has never been used in the company before

continues

Appropriate rewards:

_____

_____

V. A high-performing employee
   who likes being in charge of
   projects is frustrated because
   the company is not promoting
   people into management
   positions.

   Probable need:

   _____

   Appropriate rewards:

   _____

   _____

Answers: I. (b) 3, 4; II. (c) 1, 7; III. (d) 6, 10; IV. (a) 5, 9; V. (e) 2, 8.

MOTIVATING TOP PERFORMERS

There is no shortage of ways to recognize and reward high-performing employees, both with money and without. If you are a manager with a limited budget, remember that it is not necessarily the absolute number of dollars that motivates top performers but the knowledge that their financial rewards are substantially above average in the company. That keeps their "score" up and the equity equations in balance.

Although money is important, numerous studies show that top performers are looking primarily for challenge and recognition. According to *Harvard Business Review,* one company that recognizes this fact is the business software company SAS, of Gary, North Carolina, which depends on top-performing employees to maintain a leadership position in its field. "At SAS, the most fitting thanks for a job well done is an even more challenging project," reported an article in the *HBR.*[1] Try the following challenge-rewards for high-performing employees:

- Let these employees choose their own projects.

- Take a tip from Medtronic (see the chapter *Grow Your Revenue and Profits*) and give these employees the time and resources to work on projects of their design unrelated to their usual jobs.

■ If opportunities for promotion are few, make these employees project managers, heading up cross-functional teams.

■ Give these employees opportunities to learn new skills, both on and off the job. Then make sure they get to use their new skills on the job.

■ Arrange for these employees to attend conferences or meetings normally reserved for higher-ranked personnel.

Unfortunately, managers sometimes assume that their stars are self-motivated, and forget to nurture that motivation until it is too late and performance slips or the employee finds another job. Even top performers have been heard to grumble, "Nothing you do gets you a thank-you around here, so why bother." So be generous—but always sincere—with a thank-you, warm praise, and exposure to upper management.

Always be very specific about the behavior or outcome you are recognizing. A general "thanks for the good work" doesn't really convince your employee you've paid much attention to what he or she has been doing. You'll have a much better impact with something like this:

Thanks for the energy and long hours you've dedicated to developing the new tracking system. What you've accomplished will save us all time and money. In fact, I've just used it and gotten my answer in half the time it used to take.

That statement illustrates some keys to effective praise. So, whenever possible, include the following information with your thank-you:

■ Be specific about what you are praising.

■ Acknowledge both the effort and the outcome.

- State the impact on the organization.

- State the impact on you personally.

MOTIVATING POOR PERFORMERS

Using recognition and rewards to motivate poor performers presents an apparent paradox. Equity Equation 1 (see the chapter *Retain Your Best Employees and Recruit New Talent*) states that rewards must be equal to the quantity and quality of work done by the employee. Under this principle, high performers receive much more recognition and many more rewards than low performers. However, the low performers often need management to motivate them the most.

To motivate poor performers, you need to recognize small improvements and positive changes in processes and procedures even if outcomes aren't yet up to par. Such incremental advances hardly warrant a bonus or a testimonial dinner, but they should be rewarded with an honest show of appreciation. One of the great characteristics of the phrase "thank you" is that it is as appropriate for small accomplishments as for major ones.

Being specific is as important in motivating a poor performer as in recognizing a top performer—maybe even more so. Because your goal is for the employee to repeat and further improve one satisfactory behavior among a host of unsatisfactory ones, you need to clarify precisely what that satisfactory behavior is. If you do not clarify the satisfactory behavior, you risk validating other behaviors you are hoping to change. A general "good work today" could suggest to an employee that it is okay to come in late, talk to friends on the telephone, and misspell several words, as long as one task got done on time.

The following statement reinforces a specific behavior:

Thanks for the extra time you spent to finish the filing before you went to lunch. Because you did that, I was able to quickly find the letter from Jarvis when she called. That put me in a much better position to negotiate a better deal for us.

Notice that the previous statement contains all the keys to effective praise listed under the section "Motivating Top Performers." Yet it doesn't overbalance the first equity equation by reacting out of proportion to the employee's behavior.

MOTIVATING EVERYBODY ELSE

In between top-performing stars and problem employees, most organizations have a cadre of average workers, who meet the requirements of their jobs but seldom shine by doing something extraordinary. It is easy for a manager to focus on the stars and the problems, while taking for granted that the middle group will go on doing the same satisfactory work, day after day. However, each of those average individuals is capable of achieving a personal peak performance. Adding all those personal bests together could significantly improve organizational outcomes. It is the manager's job to coax the best possible performance out of each middle-of-the road employee. Managers have several options for recognition techniques that are particularly appropriate for inspiring peak performance among this mainstay group, including the following:

■ Work with them to set individual stretch (but achievable) goals, with the promise of defined rewards upon accomplishment.

■ Invite them to participate on a team to define the unit's rewards program (more about this in upcoming chapters).

■ Notice when they do work in support of accomplishments attributed to the unit stars. Make sure they share in the recognition.

■ Set up a high-visibility system under which employees recognize each other. They frequently see helpful things their colleagues do for each other that managers miss.

■ Invite their advice on improving the systems and processes they work with. When their ideas work, acknowledge their contributions to the whole unit and upper management. If their first ideas don't make a noticeable improvement, help them hone these ideas or develop new ones based on lessons learned.

When you use recognition and rewards to motivate an employee, whether a fast tracker, steady plodder, or underachiever, your goal is to reinforce successful behaviors so that the employee will repeat them and apply the same dedication to other tasks.

EXERCISE 2

SELF-ASSESSMENT

What have you done in the past month to inspire peak performance from at least one:

Top performer?

_____

_____

Average performer?

_____

_____

Poor performer?

_____

_____

What is one more way you could use recognition/rewards to inspire each?

Top performer: _____

Average performer: _____

Poor performer: _____

NOTE

1.   Richard Florida and Jim Goodnight, "Managing for Creativity," *Harvard Business Review,* August 2005.

PART TWO

2

TEN GUIDELINES FOR RECOGNIZING AND REWARDING EMPLOYEES

What gives a reward value in the eyes of employees? More than just its price tag. Some organizations get more mileage out of a handshake than others do with a big bonus. The difference is in how rewards are administered Your recognition and reward system will have more impact if you do the following:

- Involve employees in designing the system.

- Determine reward criteria that are both specific and inclusive of all employees.

- Make sure your rewards are in sync with stated company values.

- Recognize behaviors as well as outcomes.

- Individualize rewards—give people what they want.

- Say "thank you" a lot.

- Make it your goal to boost workers' self-esteem and their esteem in the eyes of others.

- Develop an atmosphere that fosters intrinsic rewards.

- Reward the entire team for team accomplishments.

- Develop a rewarding work environment and an enlightened work/life approach so that working for your organization is its own reward.

DETERMINE YOUR GOALS AND
GET EMPLOYEE INPUT

C heck any of the following statements you've heard in your work-place during the past year:

☐ "I don't know what you have to do to get any appreciation around here."

☐ "Why should I work harder just to get a dumb plaque (or certificate, paperweight, trophy)?"

☐ "Sure the company gives out awards, but not for anything I do on my job."

☐ "If you get an award, everybody thinks you've been ingratiating yourself with the boss [probably expressed in a more colloquial way]."

☐ "The awards are rigged so the same people get them every year."

☐ "If I tried to compete for that award, I'd never have time to get any other work done."

☐ "You can do a great job here, but still never get an award."

These statements are common signals that your recognition and reward program—if you have one—is not achieving its goals, and needs to be revisited. If you don't have a structured reward program, it is time to design one. Even if you manage only one unit in a big company, you can build a program that will have an impact on employee retention and performance and boost your group's contribution to the organization's bottom line.

EXERCISE 3

GETTING STARTED

Your first step in creating an effective recognition and reward program is to answer the following three questions:

1. What organizational values and goals and departmental objectives do you want the system to support?

_____

_____

_____

2. What outputs from your department would support organizational values and goals and contribute to departmental objectives?

_____

_____

_____

3. What behaviors by your employees would support those values, goals, and objectives?

_____

_____

_____

Your reward system needs to reinforce these things.

COMPONENTS OF A REWARD SYSTEM

To be workable, your reward system should include the following:

- A list of rewards for which employees are eligible
- Reward criteria: requirements for earning each reward
- The time period for each reward

- The process for selecting recipients
- Identification of people to select recipients
- The process for presenting rewards
- Accompanying ceremonies and celebrations

Developing such a program should be a combined effort of you and the employees who will benefit from it. The more they are involved in developing and administering the new reward system, the less likely they are to voice the complaints that opened this chapter. Nevertheless, no manager can delegate the responsibility to ensure that the reward system supports the values and goals of the organization and the objectives of the work unit. So, before you invite your employees' input into the system, define your own goals and set a number of parameters. Use the following checklist to help you get ready:

DEVELOPING A FORMAL REWARD SYSTEM: MANAGER'S CHECKLIST

Before enlisting your employees' input for creating a reward system, you need to be prepared. Be sure to:

❏ Identify values, goals, and objectives and determine what outputs from your department would support them.

❏ Select the best balance between behavior-based and output-based rewards.

❏ Identify nonnegotiable behaviors. For example, if your unit provides support on demand to customers or another department during specified hours, you may need to screen out or modify any reward criteria that tolerates lateness.

❏ Establish a budget for the system.

❏ Consider the degree to which the system should focus on exceptional versus routine tasks. Many reward systems are dedicated to recognizing efforts above and beyond individuals' job descriptions. However, employees are often demotivated because they feel underappreciated for doing their regular jobs.

❏ Ascertain new behaviors and outputs you want the system to encourage.

❏ Research successful reward systems in other organizations or in other parts of your organization and determined which elements of those systems would work in your unit.

❏ Determine the best way to involve employees in the design. Will you get their written recommendations, bring them all together in design meetings, or create a design team of representative employees? If your work unit is small enough, consider involving everyone. If you select a team, make sure it is truly representative of all functions and levels in your unit.

❏ Establish a schedule for designing the system.

The tasks included in the checklist are all preparatory to actually designing and implementing the reward system. Some of them, like the balance between behavior-based and output-based rewards, will probably be up for discussion and modification by employees. Others, like the objectives and the budget, are likely to be nonnegotiable. You can delegate some of the tasks, such as the research into other systems. However, you'll have to do most of the other tasks yourself.

> Your employees' chief responsibility is to make sure the reward system meets their needs. Yours is to make sure it meets the needs of the organization.

EMPLOYEE INPUT

Your employees, better than anyone else, know the tasks and requirements of their jobs. With their help, you can establish a reward system that not only fills their needs better than one you could create by yourself, but also has more credibility.

Let's look at the potential benefits of employee involvement. When employees have input into the reward system they are more likely to:

- Know what they have to do to earn a reward, because they've established the criteria.

- Value the reward more because they also value what it represents. Objects like plaques and trophies have no intrinsic worth. But displaying them is an acceptable way for an employee to tell the world, "I did a great job at a task I'm proud of, and my management and peers were impressed."

- Respect the reward recipients, because they set the standards the recipients met. Charges of favoritism disappear when employees are system designers and judges.

- Have the chance to create an even playing field, where everyone has an equal opportunity to win the prizes.

Employee input also helps to do the following:

- Ensure that everyone's job is covered by the reward criteria.

- Balance the criteria so that no part of a job suffers when a person sets his or her sights on a reward.

- Keep the criteria realistic.

- Widen the criteria to ensure that everyone who does a good job is recognized.

At AXA Equitable's headquarters in New York City, the giant insurance company's Corporate Communication Department has created a Corporate Communications Action Committee (CCAC). Among other projects, CCAC manages a rewards program called AXA IDOL Award to recognize one employee per quarter who has made a significant contribution to the department through exceptional job performance and/or service above and beyond the call of duty. Recipients—who are nominated by peers, colleagues or a manager—can be at any level or grade within the department, and the criteria are carefully established to specifically include people who assist projects as well as those who lead them. Final selection of recipients is made by the CCAC and the senior vice president.

Does this emphasis on employee involvement suggest that the manager should just abdicate authority? Or give up the right and obligation to direct behaviors and output in the work unit? Not at all. Even with heavy employee involvement, you'll still have plenty more to do when the design and implementation of the system get under way. Be prepared to do the following:

- Coach your employees on their roles in the process.

- Share your information, your parameters, and your own ideas and preferences.

- Facilitate the planning sessions.

- Keep the group's sights on the goal—a system that supports the organization's values and objectives.

- Ensure that the system does not become so inclusive that its impact is diluted. (If everybody gets every reward, no reward will mean much.)

- Reward the system designers for their efforts and results.

- Support your employees as they work toward the rewards they define. Give feedback, assistance, and encouragement.

- Be a press agent for your reward system and your reward winners throughout the organization. Send announcements to your boss, your peers, even the president. Get articles into your company newsletter. Get your employees all the recognition they deserve!

SPECIFY REWARD CRITERIA

Knowing her employees felt overworked and underappreciated, a manager announced a new award: dinner and theater tickets for two, to be presented to one employee each month. The first month, to no one's surprise, the award went to an employee who had brought in a half-million dollar contract.

Over the next few months, the manager found reasons to give the award to a different employee each month. But eventually it was difficult to pick out a monthly winner. To employees, it began to look as if the award were just making the rounds. To the manager, it looked as if no one cared enough about the award to put in the extra effort that would really earn it. After a while, the idea petered out and no one missed it very much.

While it lasted, the award had some positive characteristics. Anyone could win it; it went to both professional and support personnel. The recipients enjoyed it, while others didn't resent the winners because the award was not large, lasting, or public. And, initially, it felt like a genuine expression of appreciation from the manager.

What it lacked were criteria for choosing each month's recipient. Once the obvious choices were made, it was hard for the manager to pick a new recipient each month and even harder for an employee with a routine job to figure out a way to win it. Although it served as a nice thank-you for a few people, it did little to motivate improved performance because candidates did not know what performance was required to earn it.

In this situation, the outcome was fairly benign. The award faded away and things went back to the way they had always been, with no one harboring hard feelings. However, in some situations, especially if the reward is significant and the candidates are competitive, the effects of fuzzy reward criteria can be seriously damaging.

HANDLING CHARGES OF FAVORITISM OR LUCK

When the reward criteria are unclear, employees will work out their own reasons why a coworker earns a reward. Looking at the evidence from their point of view, it's easy to see why, when better information is unavailable, the two most common explanations are favoritism and luck.

Without published criteria, the person most likely to win is the one who has been able to read the manager's preferences and perform accordingly all along. Often such a person has a closer relationship with the manager and gets better assignments than do coworkers. Other employees, whose efforts don't seem to pay off as well, look at that relationship and see a teacher's pet.

Or, when all other explanations are unsatisfactory, people may attribute a coworker's success to being in the right place at the right time. "Who could have guessed that what they'd look for this year would be a product improvement? Randy sure lucked into that one." Randy, himself, will probably contribute to the impression. When he's asked how he won, he'll murmur modestly, "Just luck, I guess."

Whether the consensus of opinion is favoritism or luck, the negative impact is the same. Employees are demotivated because they can't determine the connection between effort and reward. They may even perceive that the criteria are known to a select group, from which they are excluded, which only undermines their own sense of competency and self-esteem.

Even when the winner's achievement is clear and worthy, other workers may feel frustrated. If they attribute the reward requirement to product improvement, to continue our example, those not in the business of improving products will feel as excluded as if they attributed Randy's success to favoritism.

At AXA Equitable, the criteria for nomination for the company's Corporate Communications AXA IDOL Award leave little room for charges of luck or favoritism. The criteria are:

- Consistently goes above and beyond their job description, with direct benefit to the department and/or others within the department, as well as the company at large

- Assisted a specific project/program and that assistance was a key factor in the successful outcome of that project/program and exceeded expectations

- Exemplifies innovation, creativity and enthusiasm, which directly benefits their colleagues and the team

- Excellence in work performance beyond their specific job requirements

- Contribution to more efficient or productive operations

It's not just special rewards that require specific criteria. How many of your employees know precisely what changes in behavior and output would boost their performance appraisal ratings from "satisfactory" to "above average" or to "excellent"?

EXERCISE 4

WHAT ARE YOUR CRITERIA FOR RECOGNIZING AND REWARDING EMPLOYEES?

In the left column of the worksheet below, list the ways you recognize and reward the people who report to you. Include everything from pats on the back to lunch with the boss to Employee of the Month or similar awards. In the right column, list the criteria you use to select recipients.

Rewards	Criteria Used
_____	_____
	_____
	_____
_____	_____
	_____
	_____
	_____
_____	_____
	_____
	_____
_____	_____
	_____
	_____
_____	_____
	_____

It is fine to include one or two spontaneous rewards based solely on what feels right at the time. However, if these make up the bulk of your list, your reward pattern gives no direction to employees and may be demotivating to some of them.

WHAT SHOULD THE CRITERIA BE?

The answer to that question depends on your answers to questions in Guideline 1: What are your values and objectives and what behaviors and outcomes support those values and contribute to those objectives? Those behaviors and outcomes should be specified in your criteria. You also need to make sure the criteria create an even playing field so that all employees, whatever their functions, have equal opportunities for meeting the requirements for the reward. A reward for saving money may inspire some creative cost-cutting among employees who have authority over choice of vendors, materials, and equipment. However, other employees who don't have such discretionary power might feel excluded unless the criteria clarify how they can participate.

In general, some popular bases for rewards include the following:

- Customer satisfaction

- Work quality

- Problem solving

- Work quantity

- Setting and achieving objectives

- Improving work processes

- Attendance

- Acquiring new skills

Making these specific may mean tailoring them not only to your work unit but even to the individuals within it. You could offer rewards for improving work processes, for example, and then sit down with each employee to determine what processes the employee has control over, what improvements are needed, and what this employee might do to qualify for the award. When you establish reward criteria, one size doesn't necessarily fit all, especially for noncompetitive awards where everyone who meets the criteria is a winner.

SETTING GOALS

When individuals or teams are competing against a standard, not each other, there is no reason why the standard can't be defined separately for each of them. Basing rewards on individual goals produces the most precise criteria. The best designed company-wide performance management systems and incentive pay programs are all based on specific and measurable individual or team goals. You can do the same for rewards in a single work unit.

Employees can't complain about not knowing what to do when they have personal work goals with measurable standards. The key word here is *measurable*, which is fairly easy to achieve when the goal is quantifiable: produce X number of widgets, reduce errors by 20 percent, or increase sales by a specified number of dollars. It is trickier when the goal is more subjective, such as improving quality. This is when you need to be absolutely certain that you and each employee have the same understanding of what constitutes successful accomplishment of the goal. If not, you'll have some disappointed people on your hands when reward time comes around.

You want to avoid a conversation that resembles the following one:

EMPLOYEE: I don't understand why I'm not eligible for the quality award. I met my goal of training everyone to use the new spreadsheet.

MANAGER: But their accounting errors haven't decreased. The point of the training was to reduce errors.

EMPLOYEE: But they could all do it correctly in class. I can't help it if they won't do it on the job.

With no measurement specified in the goal, the employee and manager only assumed they were operating under the same criteria for success. When you and your employee set goals together, you need to carefully compare your mental pictures of what success will look like. Make sure they are in sync.

EXERCISE 5

SETTING MEASURABLE GOALS

Which of the following goals are acceptable? Answer "yes" if you think the goal is clear and measurable or "no" if you think it is open to interpretation. If you answer no, write down the missing ingredient that would clear up the problem.

Example: Increase the number of satisfied customers by 10 percent.
Measurable? No
What's missing? A definition of satisfied customer.

1. Keep absenteeism in the mail room to under 5 percent for the first quarter of the year.
Measurable?
What's missing?

2. Significantly reduce the time required to process equipment requisitions.
Measurable?
What's missing?

3. Become competent in using the new database software.
Measurable?
What's missing?

4. Bring in four new substantial customers.
Measurable?
What's missing?

5. Train two people so that they are operating the X-20 machine with zero defects by July of this year.
Measurable?
What's missing?

Answers:

1. *Measurable?* Yes

2. *Measurable?* No

What's missing? Definitions of *significantly* and *to process.* What are the beginning and end points?

3. *Measurable?* No
   What's missing? Definition of *competent.* What level of expertise and how will it be tested?

4. Measurable? No
   What's missing? Definition of *substantial.* Does this refer to the size of the customer or the amount of the business? What numbers satisfy the requirement?

5. *Measurable?* Yes

Two essentials for goal setting:
   Line of sight—Employees need to be able to look ahead to success. Keep the goals achievable.
   Limited number—Too many goals for one reward dilute the incentive to achieve each one.
   (from Ron Dockery, director, U.S. Compensation, at Medtronic)

TRACKING PROGRESS

If your reason for establishing recognition and reward programs is to improve performance, it's not enough just to set goals for your employees and then wait until reward time to see if they've met them. Managers need to keep up with employees' progress toward goals, facilitate employees' access to resources, and guide them toward solutions to problems that block their progress. Your objective should be to have all your employees meet their goals and earn their rewards.

There will, of course, be some people who work hard but don't achieve their goals. A few people will set personal goals that are too ambitious; others may back off from their goal-driven efforts to concentrate on a different opportunity; still others may take a wrong approach to pursuing the goal. These people will miss out on their rewards, but:

■ They will know why they failed to get the reward.

■ The next time the reward is offered, they can use what they've learned to improve their chances of success.

■ They'll understand that their failure to get the reward is proof of the program's objectivity, rather than evidence of its arbitrary nature. This can increase their motivation the next time around.

DECIDING ABOUT CONTESTS

Admittedly, it is not practical to establish individual criteria for each participant when the reward program is competitive. Does that mean you shouldn't have contests? To say no would be to rule out a very large percentage of the reward programs in successful organizations.

If you want to draw attention to a new priority, announce a contest with valuable prizes for the winners. Give the contest lots of publicity, urge everyone to participate, provide numerous reminders during the contest period, and announce the winners with fanfare and celebration.

Contests generate excitement and spur on competitive people. Some people get a bigger charge out of measuring their progress against that of others than against a target of their own. If you have a large number of those people working for you, competitive reward systems will motivate them.

Be aware that, unless carefully managed, contests also have the potential of doing as much harm as good. Why? Here are three reasons:

1. **Losers.** For every winner, there are tens or hundreds or even thousands of losers—people who threw themselves into the contest, devoted their best ideas, time, and energy to their contest entries, and came up empty-handed. What the losers learn from the process is that no matter how hard they work their chances of being rewarded are very small. So after one or two tries, they say, "Why bother?"

2. **Unheralded Supporters.** For any winner, there is likely to be an anonymous support group that goes unrecognized. Think of the classic acceptance speech line, "I want to thank Tom, Dick, and Harriet, without whom this would never have happened." There are always Toms, Dicks, and Harriets, whose contributions to the winning performance don't get rewarded by the organization. What happens to their motivation?

3. **Post-Contest Letdown.** After the contest, momentum grinds to a halt. When the incentive is a one-shot prize, there is often little motivation to continue the effort once the prize is won (or lost). Even if a second contest begins immediately, the winners can't triumph again with the same entry. So employees receive incentives to chuck aside what they've just spent weeks, months, or a year developing and to start something new—just for the sake of newness.

AVOIDING THE CREATION OF LOSERS

You can have the fun and excitement of a contest and minimize its dangers if you do the following:

■ Spell out in detail the specifications on which the competition will be based. How will entries be judged against each other?

■ Make sure the criteria create an even playing field on which all employees have opportunities to compete and win.

■ Have a variety of categories and several winners.

■ Recognize all good entries, BUT

■ Emphasize that the winner was definitely the best entry and show why. Never, never announce the winner with "It was hard to make a choice. . . ." That ubiquitous statement suggests an arbitrary decision, lending credence to the "luck" rationalization. It detracts from the winner's glory without making the also-rans feel any better.

■ Honor everyone who was associated with the winning entry. Give all the support people their due.

■ Have small, frequent contests with clear criteria for entry to give more employees a chance of winning.

While contests are popular, if your rewards are overbalanced on the competition side, you might want to consider converting some of them to individually criteria-based instead.

EXERCISE 6

ALTERNATIVES TO CONTESTS

In the left column of the worksheet below are some reward programs based on contests that many companies use. In the space to the right, can you recommend an alternative, criteria-based program for each? When you are finished, you can compare your answers to the suggestions that follow:

Contest-Based Reward Program	Alternative Program
1. Employee of the Month	_____ _____
2. Productivity Improvement Contest	_____ _____
3. Salesperson of the Year	_____ _____
4. Top Team Award	_____ _____
5. Idea of the Month	_____ _____

Suggested alternatives to contests include the following choices:

■ Honor all employees who are commended by customers or nominated by coworkers.

■ Post the commendations on a bulletin board where you used to hang the picture of the Employee of the Month.

■ Establish measurable productivity improvement goals for every unit and honor all units that meet their goals.

■ Honor all salespeople who meet preset quotas.

■ Establish success criteria for each cross-functional or self-directed team, and honor all teams that meet their criteria.

■ Give a small reward for all ideas. Companies that do so find the quality as well as the quantity of ideas from employees increases. Give a larger reward for each idea you implement, and honor the employee who suggested it when the new practice achieves a predetermined level of success.

USING HYBRID REWARD PROGRAMS

Some companies have created successful reward systems that combine aspects of both criteria-based programs and competitive-based programs.

Behlen Mfg. Co. of Columbus, Nebraska, has an employee involvement program titled Awareness Is Money (A.I.M.) that is open to all employees, who are known at Behlen as Partners in Progress. At the base level of A.I.M., all Partners in Progress who *submit* ideas for Safety, Quality Improvement, and Productivity Gains are awarded Columbus Bucks, good for purchases at all members of the community Chamber of Commerce.

At the next level, all Partners in Progress whose suggestions are *implemented* earn even more Columbus Bucks. In addition, those ideas resulting in cost savings for the company—reaching preset amounts starting at $10,000 and going up—receive additional Columbus Bucks. Behlen also honors an Idea of the Month and an Idea of the Year. In just over twenty years, Behlen Partners in Progress have submitted *over sixteen thousand* ideas.

The advantage of tiered programs is that they reward more people than do single-level, exclusive programs. They give you opportunities to recognize employees who will never reach superstar status. The danger of tiers is that the existence of higher levels can diminish the luster of lower levels. You can keep the lower levels from becoming "booby prizes" by giving them plenty of publicity. Play up the lowest level as a notable standard of excellence and let the higher levels be icing on the cake.

HANDING OUT ON-THE-SPOT REWARDS

This chapter has emphasized the importance of establishing clear criteria for rewarding employees. However, there are times when you just want to honor a person spontaneously for some unexpected—or long nurtured—accomplishment or performance improvement. In fact, as noted in the chapter *Inspire Peak Performance*, occasional spot bonuses are good motivators.

At Banco Popular, one of the leading community banks in the United States and one of *Fortune*'s 100 Best Companies to Work For in 2005, employees honor each other for providing extra help and for going the extra mile: above and beyond. They nominate coworkers for Popular On the Spot Awards. People and Leadership (the bank's name for Human Resources) has gift certificates for twenty-five, fifty, or a hundred dollars. The nominator decides the amount of the reward. Awards have been given for a wide variety of efforts. One person got an award for volunteering to work over a weekend to make sure a marketing project was completed. A technical team was recognized for spending extra time to recover the data when an individual's hard drive crashed.

Another company on *Fortune*'s 2005 list, Four Seasons Hotels, headquartered in Toronto, Canada, recognizes its employees for both criteria-based and spontaneous performance. Hotels conduct frequent standards challenges, where recognition is given for consistently meeting established levels of performance standards during a specified time period. At some hotels, employees can also recognize each other with "Star Cards," for example, whenever they see exceptional performance. Star Cards can lead to awards such as restaurant gift certificates.

When management presents discretionary awards, it is critical that there is no hint of favoritism involved and that every employee has reason to believe he or she could be a winner one day. To accomplish that goal, try the following suggestions:

■ Aggressively seek out reasons to give awards. When quiet, steady employees win awards, the positive motivational impact on the work unit is much higher than when awards go to high-profile self-promoters.

■ Encourage nominations from peers.

■ Give as many awards as you can find good reasons for, while keeping the requirements high enough to retain the awards' prestige and keep it from becoming an entitlement.

■ Publicize every award, with emphasis on the specific reasons why you presented it.

Self-Assessment

Do you:

❑ Establish clear criteria for rewards?

❑ Help employees set individual, measurable goals to earn rewards?

❑ Make sure there is an even playing field so that all employees can compete equally in contests?

❑ Use on-the-spot awards for exceptional performance in special circumstances?

ALIGN VALUES AND REWARDS

———————

W hat management rewards, more than all the mission and value statements ever written, tells employees what is really important to the company.

> Be careful. You get what you reward.

When promotions and plum assignments go to people who contribute new ideas and try new ways of doing things, workers get the message that the company is sincere when it professes to value innovation and risk taking. However, leaders who proclaim the importance of taking risks might as well shout into the wind if they surround themselves with lieutenants whose only risk lies in tripping over their feet when they click their heels and say, "Yes, boss." When the company says one thing and rewards another, the troops know to take their cues from actions, not words.

There are examples everywhere of organizations that undermine their own intentions by proclaiming one value but rewarding another at both the organization-wide and department levels. Besides the high-profile trials of corporate executives charged with rewarding themselves with multimillions of dollars while fleecing their stockholders, customers, and employees, here are some other situations that will look familiar:

What the Organization Says	What Management Rewards
We value quality.	Cutting corners to lower costs.
We believe in cooperation and teamwork.	Competing with each other internally.
We encourage risk taking.	Doing things the old way.
We value diversity.	Conforming.
We want our employees to have well-rounded lives, balancing work, family, and community.	Staying late at night and coming in weekends.
We put customers first.	Keeping customer contact brief.

RESULTS OF REWARD DISSONANCE

Outmoded or ill-advised reward systems can result in unhealthy internal competition, undermining of coworkers, "doctoring" the records, or mistreatment of customers. For example:

An insurance company talks quality, quality, quality in its claims offices, but it pays its claims processors on an incentive plan that rewards them for the quantity of claims they process. Quality or quantity, which do you think it gets? _____

A chain of auto maintenance centers advertises excellent, economical service. But its incentive plan for managers is based on the number of parts the center sells. What are customers likely to get: economical repairs or unnecessary new parts? _____

(What the company got was an indictment for fraud.)

A giant corporation spends millions sending all its managers to a weeklong training program to learn new leadership skills. When the managers return to their jobs, their bosses say, "That new stuff is fine for the classroom, but back here I pay you to do things my way." How much change is likely to happen in that organization? _____

A manufacturing operation is trying to convert to a team-based structure. However, it pays bonuses to the workers who produce the most units independently. What will get the highest priority, teamwork or individual work? _____

A company encourages its salespeople to focus on repeat business, which is gravy for the company, but it pays higher commissions for bringing in new customers. Which will the salespeople concentrate on, new or repeat business? _____

ASSESS YOUR OWN PRACTICES

What rewards should you change to encourage the kind of behavior and outcomes your organization says it wants? Use the following checklist to assess your practices.

In your work unit, are you rewarding (check one of each pair):

☐ Teamwork   ☐ Internal competition

☐ Quality   ☐ Quantity

☐ Resolving problems to each customer's   ☐ Getting rid of complaints as quickly as
   satisfaction   possible

☐ Individual initiative   ☐ Doing things your way

SUPPORT THE VALUES OF THE ORGANIZATION

Most companies have values statements. They post them on their websites and circulate them widely among employees, customers, and the outside community. Frequently, these statements include words and phrases like customer satisfaction, honesty and integrity, innovation and risk taking, teamwork, good citizenship, employee development, and profitability. These are not just abstract qualities. To be meaningful, they require organizations to demonstrate them through actions and to reward employees for doing the same.

Here are some examples of companies doing just that:

■ Timberland's website states, "We care about the strength of our neighborhoods, the well-being of our environment, and the quality of life in our communities." Besides its Path of Service™ and Service Sabbatical programs described in the chapter *Retain Your Best Employees and Recruit Top New Talent*, the company makes good on its statement by giving grants to its employees to help them buy hybrid cars, which use electric motors to supplement their gas engines. Timberland also pays all expenses and gives time off for eligible retail employees to participate in nine- to ten-day environmental service projects with the Earthwatch Institute.

■ Patagonia of Ventura, California, the outdoor apparel company, is another organization that stresses its passion for the environment. In its 100 Best Companies list for 2005, the *Working Mother* magazine website highlights Patagonia's program for giving employees paid time off to work full-time for environmental nonprofit organizations and its practice of saving the best parking spots for drivers of hybrid and bio-diesel cars or carpools.

■ Intuit, which is on *Fortune*'s 2005 list of Best Companies to Work For, has a program called We Care & We Give Back, based on one of the company's stated values. When employees at the software company's Tucson, Arizona, call center decided to work together to encourage one another to lose weight, the office responded in a way that combined wellness and philanthropy by giving one dollar to charity for each pound lost by an employee. The program proved so popular that it spread to other locations. Intuit also grants employees thirty-two paid hours a year to do volunteer work. Employees can volunteer with the nonprofit of their choice, but if they aren't sure where to put their efforts, Intuit makes it easy for them by setting up programs with charities near each of the company's locations. In Intuit's Corporate Communications Department, an employee committee designed its own Values Award. Each quarter

it goes to an employee nominated by coworkers for performance aligned with the company's ten operating values.

■ Accor, with hotels worldwide, encourages employee development by giving rewards not only for learning new languages,
as described in the chapter *Inspire Peak Performance*, but also for
learning skills outside employees' own jobs.

You can support your organization's values by recognizing and rewarding allied behaviors among the people who report to you. With
the help of your employees, identify specific behaviors that demonstrate
or uphold each value, then reward your employees for behaving in
those ways. For example, if your values statement lists honesty and
integrity, then someone who admits to making a mistake deserves to
be rewarded, not vilified. (That doesn't mean releasing the person from
responsibility for correcting the error.)

VALUES AND BEHAVIORS

Below are some items that turn up on most corporate values statements, along with examples of corresponding behaviors (mostly low
key, not monumental) that deserve recognition from you when your
employees engage in them.

Customer satisfaction:	Staying calm when confronted by an irate customer
	Helping people in other departments (they're customers, too)
	Providing a little more than the customer asks for
Honesty and integrity:	Giving credit for a borrowed idea
	Correcting defects, even if others don't notice them
	Admitting to a mistake

Innovation and risk taking:	Experimenting with a new process even if the old one's not "broke"
	Volunteering for a task the person has never done before
	Contributing new ideas
Teamwork:	Pitching in and helping a coworker who is behind schedule
	Asking others to participate in a high-profile plum assignment
	Changing work habits—e.g. arrival time—to meet the team's needs
Good citizenship:	Organizing a program to tutor schoolchildren
	Participating in a road clean-up
	Coaching a company-sponsored Little League team
Employee development:	Learning a new system that will benefit the department
	Coaching a coworker
	Making a lateral career move to learn a new function
Profitability:	Seeking competent, less costly vendors
	Recycling to reduce purchases
	Seeking new markets for existing products or services

EXERCISE 7

SUPPORTING YOUR ORGANIZATION'S VALUES

Fill in the spaces below as follows:

1. List your organization's stated values.

2. List behaviors to support each value in your work unit.

3. List people who have demonstrated these behaviors (even in small ways) and deserve recognition.

Value: _____

    Behaviors: _____
_____
_____

    People: _____
_____
_____

Value: _____

    Behaviors: _____
_____
_____

    People: _____
_____
_____

Value: _____

    Behaviors: _____
_____
_____

    People: _____
_____
_____

Value: _____

    Behaviors: _____
_____
_____

    People: _____
_____
_____

Value: _____

Behaviors: _____

_____

_____

People: _____

_____

_____

BUT DO THEY KNOW WHAT THE REWARD IS FOR?

Here's a quick quiz: Assume you are a manager anxious to support your company president's broadly stated plea for more risk taking. So, you champion an employee's plan to implement a significant new work process. However, the new process is a failure, costing time and money with no measurable improvement in output. Still, wanting to continue to encourage risk-taking behavior, you reward the effort by giving this employee an opportunity to manage another innovative project. What will your other employees assume you are rewarding?

(a) Failure

(b) Your favorite employee, no matter how the person screws up

(c) Risk-taking behavior, which you have distinguished from the outcome

There is no sure answer, is there? Clearly, the reward in this type of situation has a high chance of being misunderstood. Therefore, you need to be clear about your reasons for giving a reward, especially if the reward is for a behavior, not an outcome. You can lessen the probability of misunderstandings if you:

1. Make it clear at the outset that you want people to try out new behaviors although you know the outcomes are not sure bets.

2. Enlist your employees' input as you determine what behaviors deserve to be rewarded. If they have helped identify these be-

haviors, they will be more likely to recognize these behaviors in the actions of their coworkers.

3. Distinguish between reasonable behavior that carries a risk and poor business practices.

4. Clarify the degree of risk (financial, etc.) that is tolerable.

5. Let people know that, if they stay within the guidelines of reasonable behavior and tolerable risk, you will reward the behavior regardless of the outcome.

6. Be consistent in your treatment of all employees.

CREATING ROLE MODELS

When you publicly recognize and reward an employee, you hope to create a role model for the rest of the organization. Nevertheless, for others to follow the model's lead, they need to:

1. Understand specifically, in terms of behaviors and outcomes, what the person did to deserve to be singled out this way.

2. Know how the role model's performance relates to their own jobs.

3. Be confident that they will receive similar treatment if they make comparable contributions.

To meet these three needs, you should do the following:

■ Describe the recognized behaviors and outcomes at a meeting of your group and the reward recipient. You might also distribute a written description.

■ Meet separately with each employee to jointly identify ways each person can apply parallel behavior geared toward his own goals.

■ Earn employees' trust by being consistent over time in your treatment of everyone who reports to you.

RECOGNIZE BEHAVIORS AS WELL AS OUTCOMES

W hat gets rewarded in your organization: outcomes or behaviors?

EXERCISE 8

YOUR ORGANIZATION'S REWARD SYSTEM

To determine the answer to that question, write down all forms of recognition and all rewards you can recall presenting, receiving, or observing during the past several months in the first column of the worksheet below. Your list should range from pats on the back to raises, bonuses, and promotions to big awards like Employee of the Year. In the second column, describe what the recipient did to earn it. Finally, in the third column, classify each winning performance as a behavior or outcome. For example, arriving on time every day is a behavior. A 10 percent improvement in productivity is an outcome. Responding calmly and politely to irate customers is behavior. A 20 percent decrease in the number of complaint letters from customers is an outcome.

Recognition/Reward	What Earned It?	Behavior or Outcome?
_____	_____	_____
	_____	
_____	_____	_____
	_____	

Recognition/Reward	What Earned It?	Behavior or Outcome?
_____	_____	_____
	_____	
_____	_____	_____
	_____	
_____	_____	_____
	_____	
_____	_____	_____
	_____	
_____	_____	_____
	_____	

If your organization is like most, it probably recognizes and rewards outcomes more than it does behaviors. Maybe that is fallout from our long-term romance with management by objectives or maybe it is a byproduct of the empowerment movement. From either point of view, rewarding people for specific behaviors may give the impression of trying to control behavior, rather than giving employees the right to choose their own methods for accomplishing their goals. It is also possible that concentrating on outcomes could be the inevitable result of our focus on the bottom line.

There is nothing wrong with rewarding outcomes. In fact, to do so is crucial. If you've classified all your rewards as outcomes, every one of them was probably worthwhile. However, if your organization skimps on recognizing desirable behaviors, you are missing opportunities to improve employees' perception of the equity equations; to motivate them to improve their skills, work habits and processes; and to clarify for them what behaviors the organization values.

> Banco Popular gave Popular On the Spot Awards to many employees for staffing an emergency call center in Florida during a hurricane.

By recognizing and rewarding employees' behavior, you can:

- ■ Support a culture change in the organization. If you want people in your organization to find it natural to cooperate rather than compete with coworkers, take prudent risks rather than sticking to the tried and true, and take responsibility, you must recognize these changes when you see them, not wait for an outcome to occur.

■ Sustain workers' interest and excitement about a project that has a long time frame before results occur.

■ Reward employees fairly if the outcome of their efforts is negative through no fault of their own—if someone else falls down on the job, for example, or a project is canceled because company priorities change.

■ Reinforce behavior changes made by unsatisfactory or borderline performers.

MOTIVATING NON-SUPERSTARS

The chapter *Inspire Peak Performance* in Part 1 recommended using recognition and rewards to encourage performance improvement by unsatisfactory workers. If you wait for a significant change in outcome, you may never get a chance to recognize or reward the employee you want to motivate. Without reinforcement, a poor performer is unlikely to sustain a behavior change long enough to accomplish an improved outcome.

A small gift for an employee who works through lunch one day (however reluctantly), praise for correcting mistakes without being told, a nonsarcastic thank-you for arriving on time for a change—all of these are rewards for small behavior shifts. An employee who receives reinforcement for one change may try another, and then another, until all of them add up to the performance improvement you are looking for. Eventually you may get an outcome worthy of celebration.

A Baker's Dozen of Behaviors Worth Recognizing

1. Learning new skills

2. Pitching in to help a coworker

3. Mediating a conflict

4. Volunteering for grunge work

5. Giving a customer extra attention

6. Mentoring a new employee

7. Tackling a problem in a fresh way

8. Making people laugh in a stressful situation

9. Sharing information

10. Taking notes in a meeting

11. Perfect attendance

12. Adapting willingly to change

13. Cross-training another employee

. . . and all the other behaviors mentioned throughout this book.

Many companies effectively use token awards—inexpensive gifts ranging from mugs to pens to T-shirts—to show their appreciation for helpful behaviors. When you give such awards, make sure you express your appreciation clearly and specifically in conjunction with the reward. Otherwise, you risk giving the impression that the reward is payment. The recipient's reaction in this situation is likely to be negative: "This company thinks all my work is worth is a ten-dollar T-shirt?"

But when you put the reward into its proper context, the recipient will remember your appreciation each time he or she puts on that T-shirt.

RECOGNIZING YOUR EMPLOYEES' EFFORTS

What have your employees done recently to deserve recognition even if they don't have outstanding outcomes to show for their efforts yet? If you think about it, you can probably come up with at least one situation for each employee in which the person put forth more effort than usual. How did you reward that effort? Use the following worksheet to list your findings. If you didn't recognize it at the time, what could you do now?

Employee	Behavior	Recognition or Reward

GUIDELINE 5

SPIN THE GOLDEN RULE

———————

Figuring out what behaviors and accomplishments merit recognition is just half the job of designing a recognition and reward program. Deciding what rewards to give is the other half. The most obvious approach would be to put yourself in the shoes of the people you want to recognize and ask yourself what rewards you would appreciate receiving in the same circumstances. However, choosing the best rewards is not that simple.

WHAT IS WRONG WITH THESE PICTURES?

- **Situation 1.** An administrative assistant worked through the weekend to prepare a package of presentation materials for the boss to use in a meeting with a potential client. In typing the materials, she discovered and corrected some numerical errors that would have made the boss look very foolish. Knowing that the assistant was shy and too modest to toot her own horn, the boss held a surprise ceremony at a staff meeting. Everyone toasted the assistant and insisted—despite her protests—that she make a speech about what she had done. She said little and slipped out of the meeting quickly, insisting she had work to finish up. The next day the assistant called in sick.

What went wrong? _____

_____

■ **Situation 2.** A production team put out an extraordinary effort to meet a deadline for shipping a new product. To show the team members how much the company valued their efforts, the manager arranged to have the company president take them to lunch in the executive dining room. The morning before the lunch, the manager overheard another worker teasing one member of the production team who was dressed up for the big lunch. "I can't wait to get out of this monkey suit," the team member responded, "but while you lucky guys go out for pizza we have to sit around upstairs and listen to the stuffed shirts spout off about how we're fulfilling the strategic mission."

What went wrong? _____

_____

■ **Situation 3.** As a reward for his superb handling of a complicated project, the manager delegated an especially interesting new assignment to a technician. The manager overhead this response when a coworker stopped by to congratulate the technician on his good fortune: "You think this assignment is good fortune?" the person retorted. "Then you do it. It seems to me all you get around here in return for your efforts is more work. How am I going to tell my family it's back to late nights and weekends in the office?"

What went wrong? _____

_____

■ **Situation 4.** Another manager behaved quite differently from the one in Situation 3 when an employee did exceptional work. Instead of giving the person another task to start on, the manager gave her a week off in gratitude. Every day that week, the employee showed up and hung around looking anxious and annoying others by meddling in their work.

What went wrong? _____

_____

■ **Situation 5.** A manager worked hard to win a promotion for an excellent employee whose opportunities had seemed limited due to restructuring and a reduction in management ranks. The new job meant greatly expanded responsibilities in a new facility on the other side of town. The manager was shocked when the employee expressed reluctance about accepting the new position. "I don't know," the employee said, "I like what I do here. All my friends are here. And that building is more than an hour away from where I live." The manager considered the employee ungrateful and began to question the person's future with the company.

What went wrong? _____

_____

In each of the five situations, the manager used a reward you'll find recommended in any text on motivating workers, including this one. The first manager praised the employee publicly. (You've heard that one a hundred times: praise in public, criticize in private.) The second manager arranged for the employees to have exposure to upper management. The third manager offered interesting work and the fourth an opportunity for well-earned rest and relaxation. In the fifth case, the manager arranged for the most coveted reward of all, a promotion.

So what went wrong? By now you've figured out that the answer is basically the same for all the situations. When choosing rewards, the managers failed to consider the wants and needs of the employees being rewarded. More likely, the managers asked themselves what they'd like from their bosses in the same circumstances and assumed that the person to be rewarded would be delighted to get the same thing.

"Do not do unto others as you would that they should do unto you. Their tastes may not be the same."
—George Bernard Shaw, British playwright and critic

ONE PERSON'S FISH MAY BE ANOTHER'S POISON

The value of a reward is in the perception of the receiver. And what one person considers rewarding, another may find punishing. A number of issues, some innate and some circumstantial, affect our reactions, including the following ones:

- **Personality.** In Situation 1, the manager knew the administrative assistant was very shy. That should have been a hint that she might not enjoy being thrown into such a vivid spotlight. Does this mean you should never publicly recognize a shy person? Of course not. Many people who are too shy to seek attention love it when it comes unexpectedly. What it does mean is that it's a good idea to check before forcing a person into a situation that is quite out of character.

- **Trade-Offs.** To get a presidential thank-you, the production team had to put up with razzing from coworkers, the loss of personal time (lunch with their friends), and uncomfortable clothes and environment. The manager might have been better advised to invite the president down to the shop floor to deliver a personal thank-you before taking the team out for a relaxed lunch. There are no hard-and-fast rules to guide you here. It would be a mistake to conclude from Situation 2 that no blue-collar workers like mixing with executives. The best guideline in a case like this one is to give choices.

- **Work/Life Balance.** At what point does work begin to infringe unacceptably on personal life? That varies from individual to individual. And for any one person, it can change as the person's personal life changes. When you "reward" someone with an assignment that promises extra hours or unusual travel, make it an offer that is okay to refuse. Better yet, give the person an opportunity to design a project to fit his or her own lifestyle.

- **Motivational Drives.** As you read Situation 4, you probably thought the rewards in Situation 3 and 4 should have been switched. Then the latter employee could have plunged happily into a new project. What the manager is Situation 4 failed to take into consideration was the individual's need for achievement. The manager's well-meaning gift of free time merely separated her from what she liked best. Situation 5 also illustrates the importance of personal needs. One characteristic of that employee that the manager ignored was the person's social drive. Personal relationships on the job were part of what had inspired her outstanding performance.

WHAT'S A MANAGER TO DO?

Short of mind reading, how is a manager supposed to figure out what reward will please a person and what might do harm? Following are some specific suggestions and guidelines that should help to keep you out of trouble.

- **Ask.** That is the most obvious solution. Privately tell the person you are very pleased with his or her work and explain the reward you had in mind, making it clear your idea is not yet cast in stone. Let the person know that what you really want is to give something he or she values. Then ask for a reaction to your proposal.

   One potential drawback is that the person may not be willing to respond honestly to the manager's suggestion. What you mean as an offer may be perceived as an edict, something the person must endure. Some workers have found it is better never to say no to the boss.

- **Give options.** If you give a few suggestions, the employee can pick one without fear of offending you.

- **Observe.** What makes the person smile? What does the individual take pleasure in during the workday? What does the person talk about enjoying during free time?

■ **Confirm your observations.** Sometimes it is appropriate to ask a good friend of the individual or even to call up a close family member.

■ **Avoid anything that might embarrass the person.** You should know an individual very well before presenting a joke award, staging a ceremonial "roast," putting the person on the spot with a call for a speech, or even asking the person to describe his or her accomplishments to upper management.

■ **If you make a mistake and don't get the response you want to your reward, do not make judgments about the other person's lack of gratitude or commitment to the organization.** How the employee responds to your show of appreciation doesn't change the fact that he or she did a good job and is capable of doing so again. As long as the person is in the right job, someone whose pleasure at work comes from camaraderie with coworkers can be just as productive as someone with a strong desire to move up the corporate ladder.

■ **Don't be reluctant to try again if your first reward doesn't inspire cartwheels.** You won't lose face by asking, "How can I show my appreciation in a way that is more meaningful to you than last time when I put you on the spot in front of everybody?"

ONE COMPANY'S APPROACH

Baptist Health Care, which has been on *Fortune*'s list of Best Companies to Work For every year for the past five years, knows how to please each of its employees. The organization has developed a recognition/ motivation questionnaire. Using a scale of 1 to 5, the questionnaire asks respondents to rate their agreement with statements such as "I like public recognition," "I prefer to be recognized in private," "I like gift certificates," and a bevy of similar specific preferences. At the bottom of the questionnaire, there is even a section asking people to record their favorite pizza topping, snack, and candy bar.

At first, supervisors gave it to each of their employees, who completed and returned it. People liked the results so much that the company began giving it to all new employees to fill out during orientation. Now supervisors get the completed questionnaire before a new employee even starts. And new workers come in on their second day to find their chosen snacks laid out on their desks, thanks to Human Resources.

As the title for this chapter says, when it comes to recognizing and rewarding employees, you need to spin the Golden Rule a little. Here's how it should read:

Do unto others as others would have you do unto them.

EXERCISE 10

TAILORING REWARDS TO FIT YOUR EMPLOYEES

Go back to Exercise 9 in Guideline 4 where you identified behaviors by your employees that deserved recognition. Review your ideas for recognizing and rewarding them for their efforts. Are these the most appropriate rewards for each employee? What do you know and what should you find out about each employee that could influence your decisions? Make notes here if you think another reward is more appropriate or if you need to check out your assumptions first.

Employee	New Ideas About Rewards

SAY "THANK YOU" FREQUENTLY

> "Thank you" is more important than awards. Awards are one-shot things, but "thank you" can happen over and over again.
> —A worker in a fast-food restaurant

"Why should I say thank you to workers for just doing their jobs?" You've heard this question before and maybe even asked it yourself. It is not an uncommon attitude among managers.

Yet these same people automatically say "thanks" when someone passes them the bread at the dinner table. That is just good manners.

What does this attitude say to employees? People who have been brought up to say and hear thank you in response to the smallest act of service never hear the words on the job. If you want to draw conclusions from that, you'd have to say that doing one's job is of less value to society than passing the bread or taking out the garbage. Is that the message managers want to send?

WHY IT IS HARD TO SAY THANK YOU

Whatever message they want to give, some managers just find it hard to say thank you. Their reluctance may stem from a number of different factors, including the following ones:

■ Saying thank you is not in the family tradition—the company "family," that is. We learn social manners at the knees of our parents; we learn business manners across the desk from our earliest managers. So, when we reach that exalted position ourselves, we behave as our role models did.

■ Employees don't work for their managers personally, according to one line of reasoning, they work for the company. So, it's the company's job to say thank you. The company does that with a paycheck, and that's enough. This view is a twist on the old "it's not my job" syndrome.

■ There is an argument that "If I show appreciation, they'll demand more money." But why would that happen unless the organization is convincing its workers they are inadequate as an excuse to underpay them? In fact, employees who feel appreciated often work contentedly for less money.

■ Some managers are afraid they'll appear patronizing. And, in fact, some workers protest that they don't want to be thanked every time they do something right. They too say they are just doing their job. (Remember, they were brought up in the family tradition, too.) And yet, they applaud their favorite athletes every time they score, and isn't that just doing *their* job?

When employees claim they don't want to be thanked for doing their regular jobs, it may be because the term *thanks* often sounds like the manager just noticed them for the first time. "Don't thank me for just doing my job" really means "Don't you know I do this all the time?"

SMALL WORDS, BIG IMPACT

In an organization where all the previous factors are realities, it may take a cultural revolution to introduce the words "thank you" as a meaningful form of recognition. But it is worth the effort to derive the benefits.

- **Benefit 1.** Saying "thank you" validates the importance of the work people do. Since we were brought up to show our appreciation by saying "thank you," the logical line of thinking is: "no thanks . . . not appreciated . . . not worth doing."

- **Benefit 2.** The words "thank you" are always ready for use. With this phrase, you can give timely recognition, immediately reinforcing behaviors you want the employee to repeat. We punish undesired behavior the minute we see it, knowing delayed punishment has no effect, but we wait until the end of the year to reward people with a raise or a bonus. Memory, however, can be pretty murky. Months later, it is hard to pinpoint just what behaviors are being rewarded.

- **Benefit 3.** Saying "thank you" is one reward you can afford to give for partial success. You can motivate people to do a task by rewarding incremental improvements as the person performs in a way that approximates the desired behavior. Few managers can give a bonus each time an employee arrives ten minutes closer to the mandated 9 A.M. But the manager can say "Thanks for arriving earlier than you did yesterday. I'm sure you'll be here at nine tomorrow."

"The person who works well four days out of five ought to be praised four times as often as he's dumped on. But guess what. That's exactly the opposite of what happens. The 80 percent of the time that he works well will simply go without comment because that's what he's supposed to be doing."
—Fran Tarkenton, former star quarterback in the National Football League, from his book, *How to Motivate People*

Does this mean you should say "Thanks for finishing twelve letters out of the pile of fifteen I gave you to do. The rest don't really matter." Not at all. Use your thank-yous more pointedly, to reinforce what was done right: "Thanks for doing a good job on the Johnson and Brown letters. I'm hoping to get some important new accounts with them." Follow that up the next morning with, "It's really important that all the letters go out today, so they are as timely as the Johnson and Brown letters you did yesterday."

■ **Benefit 4.** Just as you can use a thank-you to recognize incremental improvements in performance that would never rate a major reward, you can also use it to show your appreciation of routine work. Most rewards go for performance above and beyond the call of duty, but where would you be if your employees weren't doing their duties. Don't they deserve recognition for their routine contributions to your success?

■ **Benefit 5.** Generous use of the phrase "thank you" is contagious. As people begin to realize that it feels good to be on both the giving and receiving end of it, more people will use it more often, boosting morale and good relationships throughout your work unit.

EXERCISE 11

SAYING "THANK YOU" FOR ROUTINE WORK

Think of a mundane, routine, and utterly critical task done by each of your employees. List these tasks here to remind you to acknowledge the importance of this work by saying "thank you."

Employee	Task
_____	_____
_____	_____
_____	_____
_____	_____
_____	_____
_____	_____

---------------------   ----------------------------

---------------------   ----------------------------

---------------------   ----------------------------

---------------------   ----------------------------

SAYING "THANK YOU" SO IT MOTIVATES

When you thank your employees, you will underline the importance of their work and your appreciation of their efforts if you follow these three guidelines:

1. Be specific about what behavior you are recognizing with your thanks. For example,

   "Thank you for smiling at each customer and remaining calm even on hectic days. I know it gets hard sometimes and I appreciate your willingness to stick it out each day."

   "Thanks for a great job" isn't good enough. Anyone can say that, even someone who hasn't the slightest idea what work the employee has done.

2. Tell the employee why the behavior is important to you and the organization.

   "Your helpfulness and good cheer keep our customers coming back. Our business depends on return customers."

3. Be immediate. Thank your employees on the spot; don't wait for a staff meeting or a more opportune moment, such as a time when everyone is less busy. (You can say thank you at those times, too, but make those thanks in addition to the spontaneous ones.)

   "Thank you for staying calm with that customer. I appreciate that you kept smiling despite the customer's rudeness."

EXERCISE 12

WHAT ARE YOU GOING TO SAY?

In Exercise 11, you identified tasks you want to thank your employees for doing. Here, plan how you will say thanks, being specific and spelling out why the task is important. Note also when you will say it to make it as timely as possible.

Employee	What You Will Say and When

Employee	What You Will Say and When
_____	_____
	_____
_____	_____
	_____
_____	_____
	_____
_____	_____
	_____
_____	_____

BOSSES AND PEERS NEED IT, TOO

A thank-you isn't just for people who report to you. It is the reward you have the power and the resources to give to your boss and your peers in the organization when they do something of value to you. It is also a tool for influencing changes in their behavior. By thanking them specifically when you catch them doing something that is helpful to you, you give them the information and motivation they need to continue behaving in a way that is best for you.

Your boss needs to be appreciated just as much as your employees—and you—do.

GUIDELINE 7

NURTURE SELF-ESTEEM

Recognition → *Self-esteem* → *Performance*

When people are recognized for their potential, their efforts, and their accomplishments, there is a greater likelihood they will develop into employees who do the following:

- Set challenging goals for themselves

- Find innovative ways to meet the goals

- Overcome setbacks, because they assume they can

- Continually seek new opportunities

- Enjoy responsibility and managing their own work

Without that recognition, it takes unusually thick skin and exceptional inner drive not to:

- Feel inadequate and thus resist challenges

- Stick with what is familiar and low risk

■ Blame oneself when things go wrong (often covered up by blaming others)

■ Hide mistakes

■ Look for direction from others

Consider the cases of two employees who started work together in a big company. They had similar backgrounds and skills and both joined the company full of enthusiasm, with expectations of exciting, successful careers.

A few years later, Employee A was well on the way to turning those expectations into reality. This employee had a track record of applying innovative solutions to problems and confidently looked forward to every new challenge.

Employee B, on the other hand, had settled into a routine job and lived in fear of losing that if the company downsized. Turned down for a promotion, Employee B wasn't surprised. "I didn't really expect to get it," this employee told a friend.

Working in the same company, how did Employee A develop into a self-confident achiever while Employee B shriveled into a person with low self-esteem and few prospects? If you could study a videotape of their years on the job, you would see a noticeable difference in the way they were managed.

You would see that Employee A's first manager introduced A to the work unit as a person of great potential and a valuable addition to the department. And you would see Employee B, on the first day, being silently led to a desk and given the employee handbook to read.

You would see Employee A being invited to contribute ideas from the start and having those ideas treated with interest and respect. Conversely, you would see B's manager suggesting that B would better understand how the organization worked by watching and listening.

You would see both employees getting the lowliest tasks to do at the outset, but you'd also see Employee A's manager thanking A for doing them well and explaining how important they were to the success of the project. But you would see Employee B's manager accepting B's work with no comments.

As time went on, you would see A earning praise and recognition for innovative work. However, the only recognition you would see B getting would be negative feedback when occasionally something went wrong.

CYCLE OF DEFEAT

Over time, people whose best efforts go unrecognized and apparently unappreciated begin to buy into a negative perception of themselves. When that happens, their work reflects their reduced expectations.

It is hard to say exactly what is cause and what is effect in the negative cycle that results. It is entirely possible that if pressed for an assessment, Employee B's first manager would have told an outsider that B was a fine worker. However, never hearing encouraging words and getting no opportunities to shine, Employee B was destined to lose confidence and develop a negative self-image. As B's work shrunk to match that self-image, the manager's actual assessment of the employee took a nosedive, too, until it paralleled what B perceived it to be. By that time, both employee and employer took it for granted that B's prospects were limited—and so they were.

GIVING POSITIVE FEEDBACK

Employee B, unfortunately, worked for a manager who had never mastered the art of giving positive feedback, the form of recognition that has the biggest impact on employees' self-esteem. Assess your own managerial skills in the following checklist. As you read the following guidelines, check those you are confident you accomplish when you give positive feedback to your employees. Are you:

❏ **Specific?** Specific feedback tells the employee exactly what facets of the person's work are important to the company, gives information he or she can use to focus his or her efforts even more productively, and indicates you are paying attention and you care.

❏ **Realistic?** There is such a thing as laying it on too thick, and employees will recognize this and discount it. "With your drive and enthusiasm there's no reason you can't be making $100,000 in commissions next year," is less effective than "Your timing in closing the sale today was excellent. You picked right up on the slight change in the prospect's voice that showed she was ready to buy."

❏ **Consistent in your treatment of all employees?** Singling out just one employee for compliments makes that person and his or her colleagues uncomfortable.

❏ **Consistent with your known style?** Employees will distrust a manager who has been stingy with compliments in the past and suddenly starts showering people with verbal bouquets. If you are new to this, start low key and be very specific.

❏ **Faithful about follow-up?** There are both small ways and large ways to reinforce your feedback with follow-up. If you see a magazine article that is pertinent to the employee's accomplishment, make sure the employee gets a copy. If management holds a meeting on the same or a similar subject, take the employee along. If you can get him or her on the agenda as a speaker, that is better yet.

GAINING THE ESTEEM OF OTHERS

The way we see ourselves is largely a reflection of the way others see us. Therefore, it is very hard for employees to maintain a sense of self-worth if their managers and peers do not hold them in esteem. It is also very difficult for these employees to get the necessary resources and cooperation to perform well, grow in the organization, or participate productively in team efforts.

If others have low regard for an individual because that person is a poor performer, then performance is the manager's first problem. However, there are many other reasons, some subtle and some insidious, why some individuals fail to enjoy the esteem of their coworkers and management. This uncomfortable situation may exist because of the following reasons:

■   The person is simply too quiet to be noticed. The problem isn't necessarily negative regard, but rather no regard at all. This person is often overlooked.

■   There is a personality clash. A team of extroverts may jump to the conclusion that a serious, reserved person is standoffish and a not a team player.

■   The person's job is considered insignificant. Thus, a support person may be held in less esteem than a professional.

■   The employee's coworkers focus on one or two negatives. Perhaps the person once made a mistake that caused them all a problem, after which they failed to appreciate the individual's positive qualities.

■   Others are jealous. There's such a thing as too much fanfare. If a person joining a group is too highly touted, the others may band against this individual (particularly if they think his or her reputation is undeserved).

■   In a really negative environment, where everyone feels insecure, there is often a pecking order. The person may be on the bottom simply by virtue of having the least seniority or the lowliest position.

By giving the right kind of recognition both to the employee held in low regard and to the rest of the group, the manager can improve the way others view the slighted individual. The following checklist suggests things a manager can do to provide appropriate recognition.

It is important to remember that singling out a person for recognition can backfire if others have strong grievances (real or imagined) against the person. You can guard against this situation by spreading your recognition around, making sure everyone gets a fair share. Doing the things on the checklist on an ongoing basis for all your employees will help maintain morale and mutual respect among everyone in your work unit.

Building Employees' Self-Esteem and Esteem in the Eyes of Others

Check those items you've done for at least one employee during the past month.

❏   1. Acknowledge the entire team for a team success, specifying the contributions of each, including the employee whose esteem needs boosting.

❏   2. Send a note to your boss detailing an accomplishment by the employee and copy it to the employee.

❏   3. Circulate a memo detailing the employee's accomplishment to everyone on your team, emphasizing the person's contribution to the team's success.

❏   4. For a new person, publicly recognize his or her qualifications that can contribute most to your team's success.

❏   5. Put the individual on a small team project, on which the person's contributions are important to the project's success.

❏   6. Enlist the help of a "plant." Get someone who is respected by all to acknowledge specifically the individual's efforts and outputs, focusing on how they have contributed to the success of the whole group.

❏   7. At a staff meeting, ask each person to report one thing every other person there has done recently that helped the person who is reporting.

❏   8. At a staff meeting, acknowledge one thing every person there has done recently that helped you personally.

❏   9. Let the individual choose an assignment from a list of options, all of which involve working with others.

❏   10. Take your employees, one at a time, to meetings with your boss. Schedule
the person with low esteem high, but not first, on your list.

And don't forget to say thank you regularly.

EXERCISE 13

WHAT WOULD YOU DO?

What methods of recognition could you use to help solve the following problems? Choose techniques from the preceding checklist or be creative and think of some of your own.

■   **Problem A.** Chris has been a manager for several months in a research-and-development facility. Chris thinks Robert, a researcher, is being underutilized. He does routine work well, but seems to work in the shadow of his more experienced fellow researchers, who tend to shut him out of high-profile assignments. When Chris assigned an important role in a project to Robert, the senior researchers each came to Chris and objected, saying they were afraid Robert couldn't handle it and would let them down. Chris insisted that Robert have the opportunity, but the others have infringed on Robert's assignment, taking over his tasks one by one. Rather than stand up for himself, Robert has fallen back into his old role of doing the grunt work for the project team. Chris brought the issue up with the head of the facility, whose response was, "I don't know who this Robert is."

■   **Problem B.** Lee is the manager of a very close-knit work group in a company that has had some business failures in the past few years. One of those failures involved a product that was introduced with fanfare, but flopped. Lee was asked to take on Jill, an employee who had been part of that high-profile product team. "Jill did good work, but she's feeling pretty low right now," Lee's boss said. "I'm confident that in your group she can bounce back." Unfortunately, when they heard Jill was joining them, Lee's employees expressed resentment. "We may all be losing our jobs soon, and now we've got to shelter someone who helped cause that disaster," one of them remarked. They've pretty much closed ranks against Jill, although she willingly takes on even menial tasks to help the group.

■   **Problem C.** Jenny, an administrative assistant, was hired by Pat, the manager, as part of the company's program to help the disadvantaged. Pat didn't really have high hopes but was willing to try her out. Actually, Jenny surprised Pat by how quickly she learned the company's computer systems, but this evidence that she has ability makes her attitude almost more exasperating. She is often late with assignments and sloppy about mistakes. Jenny supports several analysts, and most of them complain about her constantly. Oddly, one analyst, Kim, seems to have no trouble with her and always has good reports about Jenny's work. In fact, twice last month Kim sent Pat notes, copying Jenny, commending Jenny's speed and accuracy in preparing reports.

Suggested Techniques from the Checklist
A: 1, 2, 4, 5, 9, 10
B: 3, 4, 5, 7, 10
C: 1, 2, 3, 6, 8, 9

GUIDELINE 8

FOSTER INTRINSIC REWARDS

———————

When we talk about rewards employees earn for their work, we are usually referring to things provided by the organization, the manager, or by others in recognition of the work done. These are *extrinsic* rewards.

But there are other kinds of rewards, which many employees consider much more powerful. These are *intrinsic* rewards, and they come from within the individual. Intrinsic rewards are good feelings people get from the work itself, feelings like enjoyment from the very act of performing tasks involved, excitement about confronting and overcoming challenges, satisfaction in helping others or accomplishing something worthwhile, and pride in doing a job well. These are the rewards that inspire missionaries, artists, and theoretical scientists. And these are the rewards that keep an employee working late on a project even when there is no expectation of overtime pay.

You can pinpoint the difference between extrinsic and intrinsic rewards if you think about what you get from your own job. What tasks do you do primarily because of the money or other tangible paybacks?

List three of these tasks here:

1. _____
2. _____
3. _____

What tasks do you do primarily because of the good feelings you get from doing them? List three of these tasks here:

1. _____

2. _____

3. _____

Your job, like most, probably provides you with some of each kind of reward. Without the first, you couldn't afford to stay on the job. Without the second, you'd hate it.

WHAT CAN A MANAGER DO?

When they are encouraged by their managers, employees frequently increase the intrinsic rewards in their day-to-day jobs by interjecting innovations and improvements into the accepted ways of doing things. When an Ibis Hotel employee in the United Kingdom noticed the hotel had no satisfaction-rating form for guests booking meeting rooms, she developed one for her hotel. Now she's had the satisfaction of seeing her form in use throughout the United Kingdom. A Portuguese employee suggested producing hotel restaurant menus in Braille, as well as the standard English, Portuguese, and French. Now that practice is spreading throughout the chain in Portugal.

Although managers can't hand out intrinsic rewards at an awards night, they can do a number of things to create an environment in their work units where:

■ Work is more fun. Yes, fun. Enjoyment is invigorating.

■ Employees know the work they do is meaningful and worthwhile.

■ Problems are viewed as challenges, not restraints.

■ It's okay for employees to try new ways of doing tasks and to do new tasks that interest them.

■ Employees know when they've done a good job.

In this type of environment, workers will experience intrinsic motivation.

EXERCISE 14

PAVING THE WAY TO INTRINSIC REWARDS

For each of the following questions, pick the answer or answers that offer opportunities for employees to experience intrinsic rewards.

1. To make a task more fun, would you:
   a. Start a regular Friday pizza lunch for the entire work unit.
   b. Encourage people doing the task to work in small teams to identify and implement creative new ways of doing the task more effectively.
   c. Have a monthly drawing for two tickets to an evening's entertainment.

2. To ensure that employees know the work they do is important, would you:
   a. Give a monthly bonus to the individual or team that saves the organization the most money.
   b. Trace the results of their efforts beyond their own tasks, emphasizing the impact of their contributions. Fill them in on the outcomes of the code they wrote, the reports they helped produce, or the products they made parts for.
   c. Treat employees who do routine tasks with the same dignity and respect you show those who do high-profile, creative work.

3. To encourage employees to view problems as challenges, not restraints, would you:
   a. Respond with interest and enthusiasm rather than dismay and discouragement when employees come to you with problems *and* potential solutions.
   b. Give a reward to the person who comes up with the best solution to a problem.
   c. Discourage people from telling you about problems until they are solved.

4. To demonstrate to employees that you welcome their innovations, would you:
   a. Support their ideas with resources and time and by running interference with upper management and other work units if necessary.
   b. When new ideas don't work, look for lessons the employee can apply to his or her next innovation rather than punishing the person for failure.
   c. Give bonuses to employees who develop innovative approaches for doing their work better.

5. So that employees know when they've done a good job, would you:
   a. Hold periodic progress review sessions in which they do most of the talking.
   b. Give them high grades at performance appraisal time.
   c. Give them tools to do their own quality control.

ANSWERS AND ANALYSIS

The best suggestions for creating an environment in which work is intrinsically rewarding are: 1. b; 2. b, c; 3. a; 4. a, b; 5. a, c.

Most of the other answers are not bad practices. Some of them are effective ways to recognize and reward employees, but they involve extrinsic, not intrinsic rewards. You'll see this as we analyze each question individually.

Question 1: Answer *a*, recommending Friday pizza lunches, is a good example of an idea that might well boost morale in the work unit. But, although it may make Fridays on the job more fun, it won't change the nature of the work one bit. Nor would *c*, the monthly drawing, although that might be a nice way to show your appreciation of the whole group's efforts.

Only *b*, which gives employees an opportunity to work together, which is often more fun than working alone, and to be creative, which is why many people enjoy hobbies, has the potential to make the work itself more fun.

Question 2: Answer *a* has two strikes against it in this exercise. First, it is an extrinsic, not an intrinsic reward. Second, since it is a prize for a competition, it does nothing to show the nonwinners that their work is also important. In fact, it may do just the opposite; after losing a few times, very able workers doing significant work may begin to get the idea their efforts don't count.

Answers *b* and *c* are particularly important for people in support roles, who rarely get credit for the work unit's output and who too often are treated as pairs of hands rather than as thinking people with a stake in the organization's success.

Question 3: Managers who take the approach in answer *a* set an example for their employees. By their actions they give the impression that although this problem changes things, it makes the project all the more interesting.

Answer *b*, like *2a*, is both extrinsic and exclusive. Answer *c* is just plain bad management. This approach encourages employees to hide their problems, often until it is too late to solve them.

Question 4: Answer *a* involves some management tasks that pave the way for employee success as well as intrinsic rewards. These are tasks that entail "serving" the employee. If that sounds like a twist, heed the words of Max DePree, former chair of the highly admired Fortune 500 company, Herman Miller, Inc., and author of equally admired books on management. In his first book, *Leadership Is an Art*, he wrote, "The first responsibility of a leader is to define reality. The last is to say thank you. In between, the leader is a servant."

Answer *b* reminds managers that asking for innovation but punishing people when it doesn't work sends an immobilizing mixed message. To enjoy trying new things, employees need to be free of fear about outcomes.

If you have the resources to give bonuses (answer *c*), they may be effective extrinsic rewards, but they won't improve the intrinsic rewards inherent in the work itself.

Question 5: Why does answer *a* specify that employees should do most of the talking at progress review meetings? Because, by inviting employees to tell you about specific things they are doing right, you are encouraging them to draw upon their own good feelings about their work, reinforcing their own convictions that they are doing well. To help them retain those convictions, you need to confirm them and to add your own positive feedback, as well as to help employees work out any problems that come up in the review sessions.

Answer *b*, like *4c*, is an extrinsic, not intrinsic reward.

Companies that do the best job of quality control make it the responsibility of the person performing the task. When you give people the tools to control the quality of their own work (answer *c*), you are also giving them the tools to confirm for themselves that they are doing their job well.

UNLEASHING INTRINSIC REWARDS
THROUGH EMPOWERMENT

With the power to pursue their innovative ideas, use their best skills, and make important contributions to the organization, employees also have increased potential for experiencing intrinsic rewards—feelings of satisfaction about their work. For many employees, power itself is an intrinsic reward.

But what is in all this for the manager? Doesn't empowering employees diminish their own power? Not at all. Power is not a zero sum game. Empowered employees working creatively produce a more powerful work unit, thus increasing the power of the manager.

You can expand the power of your employees, your work unit, and yourself by:

- Giving them authority to set goals, make decisions, and solve problems.

- Helping them obtain necessary resources.

- Facilitating their access to people (including you, upper management, people in other parts of the company) whose help and cooperation they need to accomplish their work.

- Providing information. If your organization is in a state of continuous change, both you and your employees may feel powerless because you don't know what is going on. You can empower yourself and your employees if you relentlessly pursue knowledge about your company's mission, plans, financial status, and progress toward meeting its goals.

ENRICHING A JOB TO INCREASE INTRINSIC MOTIVATION

AXA Equitable's Corporate Communications Department has developed a Shadow Project through which any employee can apply to "shadow" on a project in any business unit within the department. Shadow assignments are part time for three to six months, giving participants opportunities to develop new skills, such as interviewing, writing newsletter articles, producing videos, or planning meetings. The Shadow Project is an example of job enrichment—that is, increasing the scope of the job and providing more opportunities for challenging work.

By enriching jobs, you can help to create an environment where work is intrinsically rewarding. However, you need to be careful to distinguish between job enrichment and job loading, which merely enlarges the perceived meaninglessness of a job.

You can enrich an employee's job—and increase the likelihood that the person will find it intrinsically rewarding—by providing the following:

- A chance to develop new skills and demonstrate new competencies.

- An opportunity to handle a project from beginning to end, producing an output the employee can point to with pride and say, "I did that."

- Rotation into a project with high impact in the organization.

Be sure that, in the name of job enrichment, you don't just:

- Add another routine job to the existing ones. An employee who is bored with filing probably won't get satisfaction out of an additional assignment to distribute the department mail twice a day.

- Increase the amount of production expected. Don't reward an employee who can write 100 orders a day by expecting the person to write 150.

- Rotate the person to another equally boring job.

GUIDELINE 9

REWARD THE WHOLE TEAM

———————

One of the biggest changes in organizations over the past decade has been the increasing emphasis on teams to get work done. Self-managed teams and cross-functional teams have revolutionized the shape of the organization chart and the way work is done in many of the top-ranked companies in business today.

Inevitably, the focus on teams is also changing the way organizations reward their people. Traditional reward systems, which encourage individual achievement, are often at odds with the goals and the structure of teams.

When self-managed teams were still new, one national health insurance company reorganized its claims office into work teams that included claim processors, technical experts, and customer service representatives. The company expected that by putting these people together in teams, they would cooperate in finding better, faster ways to satisfy customers. The new system worked, and customers quickly expressed increased satisfaction. However, when biannual review time came around, the claims processors suffered a shock. Their incentive pay was based on the number of claims each employee processed. However, with team members helping each other, the differences in output between the fastest processors and the slowest ones evened out. As a result, several of the previously highest-paid processors saw their incentive pay plunge. When their pay dropped, so did their willingness to support the teams until the company restructured its reward system.

Other companies have also found that individual incentives are incompatible with team success. For example, Third Federal Savings and Loan, which has made frequent appearances on *Fortune*'s Best Companies to Work For list, has determined that paying commissions to loan officers undermines teamwork by encouraging hoarding rather than cooperating and by excluding the technical, marketing, and other people who contribute to each loan's success. That is why the Cleveland-based company rewards teamwork across the board with bonuses or other rewards for all.

In organizations with self-managed or semi-autonomous work teams, team reward systems have become the norm. In many companies, team rewards are linked directly to increased productivity of the team or of the organization as a whole.

> Behlen Manufacturing tracks the productivity of nearly fifty work teams, linking the measurements directly to financial results. As improvement occurs, the financial rewards are shared between company and team members, paid out monthly.

Many team-based companies have also developed ways to measure and reward teams for their achievements in improving their processes (working together, sharing information, communicating across teams, and so forth) and skills development (expanding the skills of the entire team). For companies to do that, each team must define the critical processes and determine observable benchmarks against which to measure its progress.

CREATING NONMONETARY REWARDS FOR TEAMS

If you don't control the company's purse strings, there are still plenty of ways to recognize and reward the teams in your work unit. Just as for individuals, nonmonetary rewards for teams frequently have as much impact as hard cash for inspiring team performance. If you are looking for ideas for rewarding teams, here's a list that was suggested by managers and team leaders in successful team-based organizations. As a reminder to yourself, check those items you have used and those you will use in the future.

Reward	Have Used	Will Use
• Start every team meeting with a round of applause for each new team accomplishment. Achievements don't have to be major to be worthy of acknowledgment. Solving a nagging problem, overcoming a setback, trying a new work process, doing something special for a customer or each other, or reaching an interim goal all deserve recognition.	❑	❑
• Keep track of all those small and large accomplishments and periodically revisit them, especially if the team is having a down spell. Post them on the wall or on a website. Send the list to upper management and copy team members, who may need occasional reminders that they are an effective team.	❑	❑
• Take pictures of the team in action. Post them on a wall or website. Encourage team members to add funny captions.	❑	❑
• Arrange for a thank-you visit or phone call (speaker phone at a meeting) from company top brass.	❑	❑
• Arrange for thank-you letters from top brass to go to every team member.	❑	❑
• Send letters to the team members' families, especially if the team has been putting in overtime. Describe the team's accomplishment and thank the families for their support.	❑	❑
• Celebrate reaching goals with food: breakfast or lunch for major goals, favorite snacks for interim ones.	❑	❑

BUT IS IT FAIR?

Is it fair to reward all team members the same? Do the problem-solvers, workaholics, and slackers all deserve the same reward? If they see some teammates coasting, won't the high performers resent it? Of course, these things can become issues. That is why many team-based

organizations have a two-tiered approach to compensation: team rewards for team accomplishments and individual rewards for each team
member's contributions to the team.

Reward the whole team for team accomplishments. Reward individuals for their
contributions to the team.

The term *team-based organization* covers a wide range of team so-
phistication and responsibility. In some companies, evaluating individual performance is still the manager's job. In other companies, with
completely self-managed teams, team members assess their peers based
on previously set individual goals.

Teams also recognize their members spontaneously for noteworthy
contributions. Some even have a rotating team role of *recognizer,* which
is one member whose job is to notice such contributions and celebrate
them. From a standing ovation to an impromptu party in a team member's honor, from a well-chosen gift to a letter of thanks signed by
all team members—all the individual on-the-spot rewards mentioned
anywhere in this book will work to acknowledge individual effort in
support of the team. What is worthy of being singled out? The following list will help you get started.

Reward Individuals Who:

■ Help out a teammate

■ Fill in for a teammate who needs time off

■ Solve an equipment failure

■ Learn a new skill

■ Teach a skill to others

■ Take on an unpleasant task

■ Discover a better way to do something

■ Mentor a new team member

■ Help out another team

Add your own ideas to the list here:

_____

_____

_____

_____

_____

REWARDING CROSS-FUNCTIONAL TEAMS
AND THEIR MEMBERS

Although high-profile project teams in some organizations receive significant financial rewards for their accomplishments, that is not usually the case for the myriad short-term cross-functional project teams that crisscross the formal organization charts of most companies today. Increasingly, these teams do some of their organization's most important work. If you are a project team leader or you manage team leaders, look back at the lists of rewards for work unit teams and team members earlier in this chapter. They are needed just as much in cross-functional project teams. Which ones will you use to reward the project teams and their members that report to you?

> Every year Baptist Health Care organizes a big celebration for the numerous teams throughout the company. For a favorite event, the company rents buses to take team members to the Blue Angel Airshow. Team members get T-shirts, a picnic lunch, and a day off work.

Short-term project team members frequently end up balancing two jobs: their regular jobs back in their work units and their jobs on the cross-functional teams. Frequently, the team leader is from a different work unit. Many organizations have a formal process by which team leaders contribute input into team members' performance reviews. If you are leading a cross-functional team in an organization whose performance management system doesn't formally facilitate such input, be sure to keep each team member's manager updated on the member's contributions to the team.

SUMMING UP

The following five guidelines can help you put team-based rewards to work. Check the items on which you want to concentrate:

❑   1. For a team effort, reward the behind-the-scenes workers in the same way you reward the more visible team players.

❑   2. Encourage the formation of ad hoc teams by paying nominal bonuses or presenting awards to everyone who joins a team to tackle a work problem.

❑   3. Encourage teams to write process, skill-development, and output goals. Recognize the entire team as these goals are met.

❑   4. Make team behavior a part of the basis for every individual appraisal. Be sure employees know this at the start of the appraisal cycle and know specifically what they have to do to get superior ratings.

❑   5. Train employees in peer assessment and provide teams with team-member assessment tools. Encourage employees to seek their teammates' assessment both as a guide to performance improvement and as a contribution to their individual appraisals. You can start by making this voluntary on their part.

GUIDELINE 10

GIVE THEM A LIFE

———— ▬ ————

It has been a long time since the old work/life model prevailed: the one with one breadwinner (male), one homemaker (female), and 2.5 children enjoying the fruits of their father's hard work and their mother's steady attention. It disappeared with the convergence of several factors: the loss of hundreds of thousands of well-paid manufacturing jobs that supported the model, the full-scale onslaught of women into the workforce, and the emergence of family units that bore little resemblance to the $1 + 1 + 2.5$ group. Added to those social factors were on-the-job pressures that included the push for ever-greater productivity; the twisting, bending, and upending of the traditional top-down organizational structure in response to the productivity press; and the boom in technology that changed not only the jobs people did, but how and where they could do them.

What emerged from that mix, besides a bunch of exhausted people desperately trying to juggle growing demands both at work and in their personal lives? One thing was a new generation of workers who looked at what was happening and said, "Give me a life." Another thing was the realization by employers that they could tap and retain smart, enthusiastic employees by providing a workplace that was hospitable as well as invigorating and by making it possible for people who were committed to their careers to participate fully in life outside of work as well. Giving employees a life takes place on both fronts.

LIFE AT WORK

■ **Work Itself.** How can you make work rewarding? If you give workers more control over what they do and encourage innovation, they'll find ways to work that will reward both them and the organization (not to mention the customers). Wegmans, a regional supermarket chain in the eastern United States, topped Fortune's 2005 list of Best Companies to Work For. It empowers its workers to do exceptional things for customers. *Fortune* reports that one employee sent a chef to a customer's home, and another arranged for the store to cook a turkey for a customer who had bought a bird too big to fit into her oven. Having power to do the extraordinary breathes life into even routine jobs.

■ **Work Conditions.** Flexible work schedules, telecommuting, and job sharing smooth the transitions between work and personal life for millions of workers. The possibilities range widely. Flextime can mean adjusting the workday's start and end times to accommodate outside responsibilities, or it can mean giving people freedom to come into the workplace whenever they want—night or day. It can also mean compressing a full workweek into a fewer number of days. Telecommuting can mean taking a laptop home for a day to supervise the plumber, or it can mean working from home all the time. Job sharing isn't as common yet, but it allows some people to work part-time in jobs that require a full-time presence.

■ **Workplace Amenities.** If it makes life easier and work less stressful, why shouldn't workplaces be just as pleasant as possible? On-site fitness centers have been growing in popularity for years. Lactation rooms for new mothers are popping up in corporate offices. Big corporate campuses have on-site, subsidized child-care facilities, frequently offering a reasonable number of free or inexpensive backup care days for parents who are unexpectedly stuck without a sitter. On a smaller scale, some companies keep games and videos around so that parents can simply bring their kids to work on snow days or school holidays.

Many companies have programs whose purpose is simply to interject fun into the workplace. They look for ways to celebrate, like having baby showers for expectant mothers and fathers. Baptist Health Care facilities each have an Employee Satisfaction Team that plans festivities like barbecues and punch-and-cookie parties. The teams also keep party carts on hand, filled with balloons, hats, and inexpensive gifts, ready on the spot when any unit has something to celebrate. Third Federal Savings and Loan has employee contests that are just for fun, such as ice cream–eating competitions. In 2005, Third Federal staged a mural contest, inviting employees to submit samples of their work. Two winning artists translated their samples into large-scale works on the headquarters' walls.

■ **Health Initiatives.** In the good life that we imagine for ourselves, we enjoy fitness and vigor. Smart companies reward their employees with opportunities to improve and maintain their health. On its website, HSBC of Prospect Heights, Illinois, an international financial services company, reports that it contributes a hundred dollars to the healthcare flexible spending accounts of employees who participate in Health and Wealth, its free health-screening program.

The initiatives that employees respond to most enthusiastically are frequently those related to weight loss, smoking cessation, and exercise. For example, Third Federal Savings and Loan offers employees a thousand dollars if they stop smoking for a year. It has sponsored walking contests, giving duffle bags and bragging rights to winning teams. As described earlier in the book, Intuit gives one dollar to charity for every pound lost by its Tucson call center employees who choose to participate in a local wellness program.

> If you can't give your employees a thousand dollars to stop smoking, what about dinner and a movie or an office gala in their honor?

Although most of the programs described in this chapter are company-wide initiatives, many of them can be scaled down for implementation in individual work units. You may not be able to authorize murals in the company cafeteria, but you could sponsor a show of employee art framed and displayed on your walls. If you think about it, you can probably come up with a low-budget version of most of the ideas discussed here.

EXERCISE 15

THE GOOD LIFE AT WORK

In addition to the list in the worksheet below, check those programs already in place in your organization, and record your ideas for similar programs you can do on your own. This is a list of sample programs; it is far from all-inclusive. Add others you know about at the bottom.

Programs That Improve Life at Work	Currently in Effect	What I Could Do
Workers given more control over their work	❏	_____
Encouragement of innovation	❏	_____
Flextime	❏	_____
Compressed workweek	❏	_____
Telecommuting	❏	_____
Job sharing	❏	_____
Fitness center	❏	_____
Lactation room	❏	_____
Help with child care	❏	_____

Baby showers for moms and dads	❏	_____
Team to plan festivities	❏	_____
Party cart	❏	_____
Fun contests (e.g., ice cream eating)	❏	_____
Mural contest	❏	_____
Incentives to stop smoking	❏	_____
Weight-loss incentives	❏	_____
Walking contest	❏	_____
Incentives to participate in wellness program	❏	_____

Others:

_____	❏	_____
_____	❏	_____
_____	❏	_____
_____	❏	_____
_____	❏	_____

EXERCISE 16

THE GOOD LIFE OFF THE JOB

Progressive companies realize that giving workers the time and resources to be with their families and to pursue outside interests not only boosts employee loyalty but develops more skilled, better rounded individuals who have more to contribute at work.

The worksheet below lists several ways companies provide that kind of reward, from nontraditional family support policies to paid time off for volunteering. Just like the worksheet in Exercise 15, this worksheet has spaces for you to check those rewards offered by your organization and to translate them into rewards you can offer people who report to you.

Programs That Improve Life Outside Work	Currently in Effect	What I Could Do
Paid time off for volunteering	❏	_____
Paid time off for children's school activities	❏	_____
Paid paternity leave for fathers and domestic partners	❏	_____

Programs That Improve Life Outside Work	Currently in Effect	What I Could Do
Paid adoptive leave	❏	_____
Grants toward adoption expenses	❏	_____
Monetary awards for foster parents	❏	_____
Extended leaves for pursuing volunteer interests with job guarantee and no loss of promotability upon return	❏	_____
Elder-care, as well as child-care subsidies	❏	_____
Reimbursement for child care during business trips	❏	_____
Paid leave in cases of extreme emergency	❏	_____
Parents' Night Out free babysitting	❏	_____
Others:		
_____	❏	_____
_____	❏	_____
_____	❏	_____
_____	❏	_____
_____	❏	_____

PART THREE

3

150 WAYS TO RECOGNIZE AND REWARD EMPLOYEES

Although the list of 150 specific suggestions for ways to recognize and reward people is not exhaustive, it should include some ideas that you will find useful and others that will spark new ideas of your own. Many of these ideas have been mentioned elsewhere in the book, while others you will encounter here for the first time. Some are free (in monetary terms), many have a nominal cost, and a few are fairly expensive or open-ended (the dollar amount being up to you). All of them are intended to supplement your organization's compensation plan. Scaled up or down, most of these ideas are applicable to any size work unit.

Most of the items on the list are geared for managers to give to employees, either individuals or teams. However, the people who work for you aren't the only ones who deserve recognition. Therefore, some items are for coworkers, customers, and even your boss. A few are for people not on your organization's payroll, but brought in under contract to work on short- or long-term projects.

To make the list easier to navigate, it is divided into sections under the following titles:

- Rewards for Accomplishing Preestablished Goals

- Regularly Scheduled Recognition Events

- Contests

- Ongoing Reward Programs
- Privileges
- Work Adjustments
- Recognition That Doesn't Cost Money
- Trophies and Gifts
- Broadcasts
- Team Specials
- Special Events
- Day-to-Day Feedback
- Lifestyle Rewards
- Peer-to-Peer Recognition
- Recognition for Bosses, Customers, and Contractors

THE 150 WAYS

As you review the following list, note those items you have used and those you will use (not necessarily mutually exclusive). If your have-used count is high, you'll want to keep it up. If it is low, that might be your cue to put more checks into the "will use" column and follow up on your intent.

Reward	Have Used	Will Use

REWARDS FOR ACCOMPLISHING PREESTABLISHED GOALS

1. Cash bonus upon goal accomplishment by an individual or team. Don't wait until the end of the year when the reward's connection to the work effort has worn thin. _____ _____

2. Set a measurable work unit goal for a specified time period and celebrate when your unit achieves it. _____ _____

3. Wall of fame. Keep it active for a year, adding framed pictures of employees or teams as they complete written goals. _____ _____

4. Recognition for completing college degree under company's tuition reimbursement plan. This suggestion comes from JonScott Williams, organization development consultant at Wyeth Pharmaceuticals in Richmond, Virginia. Start with a congratulatory letter from you and/or company executives. Add a gift or a night on the town if you wish. _____ _____

5. Recognition lunch, honoring people for meeting short-term (monthly, quarterly) goals. _____ _____

6. Announce a day-, week-, or month-long challenge for anything   _____   _____
   from cleaning the storage room to cleaning up a backlog. See
   Trophies and Gifts or *Recognition That Doesn't Cost Money* for
   suggestions of ways to honor everyone who contributes effort and/
   or successful ideas.

REGULARLY SCHEDULED RECOGNITION EVENTS

7. Values lunch (or breakfast or even dinner) to recognize specific   _____   _____
   behaviors by employees that support your organization's stated
   values. Enlist nominations from coworkers (requiring specific
   descriptions of behavior) in advance and recognize everyone
   nominated.

8. Thank-you meeting, at which everyone in work unit thanks   _____   _____
   everyone else for something specific. Hold these at regular
   intervals and remind people to keep track of small favors that they
   can mention when called on to speak.

9. Suggestion plan prizes. Reward each contributor with a chance for   _____   _____
   a monthly drawing. Have several prizes of different values each
   month. If you are afraid people will stuff the suggestion box with
   worthless ideas, you needn't worry. Organizations that pay for
   every suggestion regardless of whether or not it is implemented
   report that the quality of the suggestions goes up, not down. You
   can also maintain a level of psychological control by reading aloud
   every suggestion that wins a prize.

10. Biggest Blunder Award, given monthly to the person who admits to   _____   _____
    the biggest mistake. It can be a funny trophy but the intent is
    serious. In too many organizations, people are afraid to admit their
    mistakes, so they get covered up, not solved. The presentation
    event should be followed up by a problem-solving meeting, and the
    outcome should be a viable approach to resolving the problem.
    Start by giving yourself the award and asking others' suggestions
    for tackling your problem. Then invite others to nominate
    themselves for the award next time.

11. Solution Award, presented as a follow-up to the Biggest Blunder   _____   _____
    Award when the mistake is corrected.

12. "Catch Them Doing Something Right" video or DVD. Capture a   _____   _____
    year's worth of on-the-job highlights and play them at a recognition
    event or holiday party. Then keep it ready to play in the work unit
    all during the following year.

13. Work unit yearbook or "annual report" featuring accomplishments   _____   _____
    of all employees. Desktop publishing makes it possible to do a

professional-looking job inexpensively. Each employee gets one. Keep yours in a prominent place in your office.

CONTESTS

14. "Who can do the most *(fill in the blank)* in a week?" contest. Appropriate prizes: dinner and a movie, catered dinner for the family at home, or—at no cost—the manager washes the winner's car in the company parking lot. Keys to success: a level playing field on which everyone starts with a perceived equal chance at winning; a short duration; a prize that's worth competing for, but is not an incentive to undercut coworkers nor likely to cause jealousy.

15. "Design a logo" contest. This one is for boosting morale and work unit spirit. An appropriate prize: have a graphic artist render the logo and frame a large and small version. Hang the large one in a public place and present the small one to the winning designer.

16. Mural contest. Copy Third Federal Savings and Loan's idea (mentioned earlier in the book) and invite employees to submit samples for judging. Winners get to paint the walls.

17. Walking contest, especially good for employees who sit all day. Employees can compete on trails or treadmills. They can do it in teams or as individuals. Give the winners a choice of prizes from a sports catalogue.

ONGOING REWARD PROGRAMS

18. Department Recognition Board. Post citations, thank-you letters, customer commendations, and notes about each other. Solicit new items as needed to keep the board full and the turnover frequent enough so the board remains interesting.

19. Create a point system, whereby employees can accumulate points in a variety of ways and use them for a choice of awards. Carlson Companies give Gold Points for, among other things, acts that support company strategies.

20. Frequent helper points. Employees accumulate them by earning thank-you notes from coworkers. Give prizes for garnering a set number of points. See *Trophies and Gifts* for suggestions of appropriate prizes.

21. Frequent overtime points. These are accumulated in the same way as frequent helper points but are earned by working extra hours. Both exempt and nonexempt employees should be eligible.

22. Custom tailor awards to employees' individual tastes. Follow the
    lead of Baptist Health Care and give all employees a questionnaire
    about their preferences.

PRIVILEGES

23. Provide a coach. Fast trackers appreciate the extra attention and
    the extra boost toward their next career goal. Executive Coach Pat
    White of Nashville, Tennessee, says she gets hired as a bonus for
    high-ranked people in organizations.

24. Do an employee's job for a day. One day just before Christmas,
    visitors to a neighborhood bank in New York were surprised to find
    that all the tellers were unfamiliar. A discrete inquiry revealed that
    management had taken over the tellers' jobs for the day. You don't
    need to wait until Christmas.

25. Morning coffee every day for a week hand-delivered by the
    manager.

26. Three-hour lunch break. Great for holiday gift shopping but a nice
    surprise when spring flowers are in bloom, too.

27. Choice of late arrival or early leave-taking. Especially appropriate
    as a reward for putting in long hours.

28. A whole day off.

29. Two hours of personal phone calls—preferably not all at once.

30. A work-at-home day. Don't make a big deal of it. Rather, say
    something like, ''Listen if you'd be more comfortable finishing this
    up at home, go ahead. We'll cover the phone for you.''

31. Grab bag of privileges. Print the ones listed above (and others you
    think of) on ''gift certificates'' and let the recipient draw or select
    one.

WORK ADJUSTMENTS

32. Increased authority. Empower the employee to take actions without
    your permission and (within boundaries) make monetary decisions.

33. Designate the person as a project leader and give her the
    opportunity to select other members of the team.

34. ''Pick your project.'' Allow the individual to determine the next
    assignment he will work on, within a predefined budget.

35. Shadow Project. Follow the lead of AXA Equitable's Corporate
    Communication Department and arrange for employees to spend

time observing and working on a project outside their own realm of expertise.

36. Job rotation. Allow employees to expand their skills and experience by spending six months in a different job.

37. "Do it your way." A reward for the rebel in your group who always thinks there is a better way. Perhaps there is. Give the person a chance to try, backed up by reasonable resources.

38. A day to work on a favorite task only. Arrange for coverage of the employee's other tasks so that the person doesn't return to a backlog the next day.

39. "Pick a job for a day." A day for the person to work at the job of his or her choice, along with or instead of the person who normally does it. Obviously, this needs the collaboration of everyone involved.

40. Recognize a team accomplishment by designating that team a consultant to other teams. Team members get the honor and others get the benefit of their skills. You may want to arrange for them to have some training in internal consulting skills.

41. "How Can We Help?" Day. This is a way for a whole team or work unit to show esteem for an overburdened and under-recognized coworker. Each person offers to assume one task for the person being recognized.

RECOGNITION THAT DOESN'T COST MONEY

42. Start every work unit meeting with praise for accomplishments and behaviors since your last meeting.

43. Write a letter to the employee's family, expressing your appreciation for extra hours the employee has given to the job, and explaining specifically what he has done and what it means to you and the company.

44. Set up a thank-you call from the president of the organization.

45. Arrange a visit from the president to acknowledge the contributions of an individual or your whole work unit.

46. A thank-you letter signed by everyone in the work unit, framed if you wish. Especially appropriate for under-recognized support personnel.

47. "I stole _____'s idea and I'm using it," certificate. Raychem Corporation created this idea years ago to encourage

people to capitalize on each other's work—to "steal" from each other. It's still good today.

48. "I had an idea and _____ is using it," certificate. A companion to the previous item. This one goes to the person who came up with the idea in the first place.   _____ _____

49. "World's Best _____" certificate. Fill it in appropriately on the spur of the moment.   _____ _____

50. Solicit customer commendations for employees and display them prominently. All Sport Poughkeepsie/Ulster Health & Fitness Centers in New York State encourage members to write citations for employees who go beyond the call of duty. Members write their citations on yellow note cards and drop them into prominently displayed big glass jars.   _____ _____

51. Ring a bell and make an announcement when someone accomplishes a personal goal.   _____ _____

TROPHIES AND GIFTS

52. Thank-you paperweight. A note signed by you and the rest of the work unit, embedded in Lucite.   _____ _____

53. Establish and name an award after an employee. If you create a Jane Doe Award for exceptional customer service, you honor Jane Doe again each time you present it to someone else. Caroline Meeks suggested this idea in *Small Business Reports*, in December 1991, and it's still appropriate today.   _____ _____

54. Take a tip from Patti Dowse of Erda Leather and bring in a massage therapist to do chair massages—especially for employees who sit hunched over machines or phones.   _____ _____

55. Donation to the employee's favorite charity in the employee's name.   _____ _____

56. Gifts of your company's products—e.g., a cartful of groceries for supermarket employees.   _____ _____

57. Membership, in employee's name, in public television or radio.   _____ _____

58. Bottle of champagne sent to the employee's home.   _____ _____

59. Bouquet of flowers delivered to the office or home. Don't save this for women only; men like flowers, too, and they seldom get them.   _____ _____

60. Framed photograph of the employee with the organization's president.   _____ _____

61. Gourmet gift. Tailor it to the recipient's tastes: fancy coffee for a   _____   _____
    caffeine addict, expensive chocolate for a chocoholic, basket of
    organic fruit for a health fanatic.

62. T-shirts, hats, mugs, etc. with the department logo. Great contest   _____   _____
    prizes.

63. Silver or gold-plated pen with the company or department logo.   _____   _____
    This is especially appropriate as recognition for an assignment
    involving heavy writing.

64. Subscription to a professional magazine.   _____   _____

65. Book on a topic related to the recipient's work or future career   _____   _____
    plans. Be sure to inscribe it with your thanks for a specific job well
    done.

66. Lottery tickets.   _____   _____

67. Instant scratch-off cards. Have them made up to reveal surprise   _____   _____
    gifts.

68. Tickets to movies, theater, or sporting events.   _____   _____

69. Dinner for two at a restaurant of the recipient's choice.   _____   _____

70. Weekend at a country inn for an individual and a companion.   _____   _____

71. Puzzle Award for problem-solvers. Give Tavern puzzles—those   _____   _____
    maddening metal rings you have to disengage.

72. Aiding and Abetting Plaque. An award to recognize employees who   _____   _____
    give their time, effort, and expertise freely to help others.

73. Autographed picture of the recipient's favorite entertainment or   _____   _____
    sports personality.

74. New furniture or wall art. Particularly impressive in a company   _____   _____
    where these require high-level approval.

75. Framed cartoon related to the work done by the recipient. Keep   _____   _____
    your eyes open and build up a collection of clipped cartoons that
    you can use for this purpose. (Try going online to a website such
    as the *New Yorker,* www.newyorker.com.) This kind of reward says
    you care and that you really understand the person's job.

76. Gift related to the recipient's hobby. Call a family member or close   _____   _____
    friend to find out what the person wants. Otherwise, let the
    recipient choose from a catalogue. Be cautious, it's easy to
    misjudge and get something that is too complicated, too
    unsophisticated, or a duplicate of what the person already has.

77. Gift certificate for a neighborhood specialty store related to the person's hobby. This is a way to build community relations, too.   _____ _____

78. T-shirts emblazoned with the employee's picture (at work) sent to members of the employee's family.   _____ _____

79. A gift certificate for lunch at a local restaurant for the recipient and a coworker in the same or another work unit.   _____ _____

80. The vault: a cabinet of various gift-awards. When you want to recognize someone on the spur of the moment, let the person choose. The ticket to the vault should be a letter or certificate that spells out the person's accomplishment.   _____ _____

81. A selection of small gifts that any employee can present to any other employee to say, "Thanks, you really helped me." Accompany each gift with a certificate that the giver fills out, specifying the actions of the receiver that won recognition.   _____ _____

82. A catalogue of logo-engraved awards that recipients can choose from.   _____ _____

83. Star pins for customer contact people to pin on their name badges. All Sport Health & Fitness Centers give them to employees for achievements like memorizing customer names as well as for years of service. A special one for teamwork has a tiny star at the end of each point of the main star.   _____ _____

84. Starfish pins. All Sport gives these to employees for acts that make a difference, such as getting a struggling exerciser to smile and have more fun. They are reminders of the starfish story by Loren Eisley about the man who walked along the beach as the tide went out throwing stranded starfish in the ocean so that they wouldn't die. Asked what difference saving a few could make when there were miles of starfish-strewn beaches, the man rescued another starfish and replied, "It made a difference to that one."   _____ _____

BROADCASTS

85. Arrange to have an article in the organization's newsletter describing the accomplishments of an employee or your work unit.   _____ _____

86. Instead of an article, write an "ad" for the newsletter, touting your unit and the people who work in it and saying what it can do for other parts of the company.   _____ _____

87. If your company has an in-house video program, get the producers to do a feature on your group's latest accomplishment.   _____ _____

88. Have a website with updates of accomplishments on your company's intranet.

89. Embellish your website with smart or funny quotes from your employees and pictures of them at work.

90. Place an ad in a local newspaper, paying homage to your employees. This is another idea from Meeks in *Small Business Reports,* December 1991.

91. An acknowledgement of an employee's accomplishments broadcast widely in e-mail.

92. An announcement of an employee's accomplishments to the person's customers, either external or internal.

TEAM SPECIALS

93. Host a pizza or champagne party to honor a team upon goal accomplishment.

94. Broadcast the news throughout the organization when a team achieves a goal.
Do the same when:

95. A team develops a process that is applied or adapted in other parts of the organization.

96. A team successfully uses an existing system or process in a new way.

97. Team members acquire and use new skills to move the team project forward.

98. Team members take skills acquired on the team and apply them successfully elsewhere.

99. New teams are spun off to perform work inspired by the team being honored.

100. Work done by the team leads to projects in other work units.

SPECIAL EVENTS

101. Cook lunch for your unit and bring it to the workplace.

102. Keep a party cart ready with balloons, hats, snacks, and small gifts for everyone, ready for a spur-of-the-moment celebration. This idea comes from Baptist Health Care and was mentioned earlier in the book.

103. Track a host of measurements and celebrate them all: reduced absenteeism, reduced lateness, reduced sick days, days without on-the-job accidents.

104. Organize a car-wash day when all the managers wash employees' cars. Who gets their car washed could be determined by a lottery.

105. Breakfast for another work unit hosted by your group. It could be bagels or a full buffet. Take it to a department that does a service for yours.

106. Take an employee to lunch in the executive dining room. If your organization doesn't have one, arrange an outside lunch in the company of a group of executives.

107. Give a high-performing team a budget to host a party for another team.

108. Send an employee to a professional conference related to his area of accomplishment.

109. Send an employee to a training course or seminar of her choice.

110. Take an employee with you to a senior level conference or meeting.

111. Take an employee to an out-of-town trade show.

112. End a workday early and take everyone to a movie.

113. "This Is Your Life." Surprise an employee with a celebration recalling the highlights of the person's career. Bring in old friends, early managers, and executives.

114. "This Is Your Life" scrapbook, for someone who would be embarrassed by the attention if you held a celebration.

115. Arrange for a team to present the results of its efforts to a group of upper-level management.

116. Create a photo collage of your employees at work and present it to your boss. Make sure in advance that your boss will display it, and arrange for your people to see it displayed.

DAY-TO-DAY FEEDBACK

117. "Thank you for _____," spoken aloud, publicly or privately (or both). Be very specific.

118. "You did a good job on _____." Again, just say it, specifically.

119. A handwritten thank-you note to an employee, with a copy in the person's personnel file.

120. "I couldn't have done it without you" certificates, for everyone to give to anyone.

121. Small bulletin boards, designed to encourage people to "brag" a little by posting their commendations or thank-you notes. Put a note from you on each board as you present it.

122. A thank-you letter to an employee's family, thanking them for their sacrifices while the employee has been working extra overtime.

LIFESTYLE REWARDS

123. Work schedules that accommodate the person's personal life such as flextime, compressed workweek, or job sharing.

124. Telecommuting, at least some of the time.

125. Community service recognition event. Give a certificate or plaque to everyone who fulfills a commitment to community service.

126. Paid time off (hours, days, or months) for volunteering.

127. Paid time off for children's school events.

128. Free baby-sitting for special occasions.

129. Paid leave for new fathers and new adoptive parents.

130. Paid time off for new grandparents.

131. Paid leave for emergencies.

132. Reimbursement for child- or elder-care during business trips.

133. Recognition—monetary or celebratory—for foster parents.

134. Baby showers and baby gifts for dads and domestic partners as well as moms.

135. Weight-loss incentive. Take a tip from Intuit (described earlier in book) and donate one dollar to charity for every pound employees lose. You could set a specified time period or make it ongoing with quarterly weigh-ins.

136. Reward for stopping smoking. As mentioned earlier, Third Federal S&L gives employees a thousand dollars if they stop smoking for a year. If that's too rich for your blood, pare it down, give a nice gift, or have a celebration.

137. Reward your employees for choosing hybrid or other energy efficient cars. If you can't give a grant toward their purchase as Timberland does, follow Patagonia's lead and give them prized parking spots.

138. Subsidized fitness club memberships.

PEER-TO-PEER RECOGNITION

139. Have employees nominate coworkers for employee of the month or year.

140. Commendation-from-peers party. Invite submissions in advance and use them all. Celebrate with cake or champagne.

141. Swap a task. Reward a coworker with an offer to trade for a day (or week) a task of yours the person covets for one of his or hers the person dislikes.

142. Blank thank-you notepads for everyone to encourage people to send them to each other. Put a thank-you message from you to each recipient on top.

143. A thank-you note to one of your peers, copying the person's manager.

RECOGNITION FOR BOSSES, CUSTOMERS, AND CONTRACTORS

144. A hand-written thank-you note to your boss.

145. A letter to your boss signed by everyone in your unit for help on a specific project or a year's worth of support.

146. "Thank a Customer" party. Everyone invites a favorite customer (external or internal) and presents a citation to the guest. Inviting the guests to respond is a great way to solicit some positive feedback.

147. Recommend your contractors to other managers in your organization.

148. Invite contractors to staff meetings.

149. Vendors' Night: happy hour for staff and contractors. This suggestion comes from Karen Massoni, an organization development consultant in private practice in New York City. One of her clients holds them monthly.

150. Send a vendor a letter of appreciation—the old-fashioned kind, not e-mail. The letter becomes a marketing tool.

REVIEW

SELF-ASSESSMENT AND ACTION PLAN

How often do you use the techniques covered in this book? Assessing your own behavior is a good way to pinpoint areas in which you might want to work harder to recognize and reward people in your organization. The items in the following checklist are culled from throughout the book. How often do you perform them?

A SELF-RATING CHECKLIST

Do You . . .	Never	Occasionally	Regularly
1. Make an effort to provide a total package of recognition and rewards that employees perceive as being equal to the value of their efforts?	_____	_____	_____
2. Differentiate sharply between top performers and average ones when you give monetary rewards?	_____	_____	_____
3. Try to understand what needs drive your employees and motivate them by providing rewards that meet those needs?	_____	_____	_____
4. Reward high performers with new challenges and opportunities to innovate?	_____	_____	_____

Do You . . .	Never	Occasionally	Regularly
5. Recognize small improvements in the behaviors and outputs of poor performers?	_____	_____	_____
6. Consistently reward behaviors that support the organization's stated values?	_____	_____	_____
7. Offer criteria-based rewards?	_____	_____	_____
8. Get input from employees regarding what rewards and reward criteria would best meet their needs?	_____	_____	_____
9. Ensure that all the people who report to you know what they must do to earn rewards?	_____	_____	_____
10. Track employees' progress and guide them to overcome obstacles as they work toward accomplishing their goals?	_____	_____	_____
11. Use competitions mostly to generate excitement about one-shot events, rather than to spur ongoing performance improvement?	_____	_____	_____
12. Recognize behaviors as well as outcomes?	_____	_____	_____
13. Make an effort to reward people in a way they value, rather than give rewards that appear valuable to you?	_____	_____	_____
14. Say thank you for routine work and incremental improvements?	_____	_____	_____
15. Say thank you to your boss and peers, too?	_____	_____	_____
16. Make sure you are very specific about the behaviors and outcomes you are praising when you give positive feedback?	_____	_____	_____
17. Enrich employees' jobs to make them interesting and challenging?	_____	_____	_____
18. Reward team members equally for team accomplishments and separately for their individual contributions to the team?	_____	_____	_____
19. Reward solving problems rather than covering them up?	_____	_____	_____
20. Look for ways to help employees achieve a work/life balance?	_____	_____	_____

ACTION PLANNING

Throughout this book, you've been invited to make notes on ways to improve your own methods of recognizing and rewarding people in your organization. Look back at those notes and at the items you marked "never" or "occasionally" in the preceding checklist. From the information you've collected, identify three high-priority things you'd like to do right away to make better use of recognition and rewards to motivate people to reach peak performance and to let them know how much you appreciate them.

Record those three action steps here.

1. _____
   _____
   _____

2. _____
   _____
   _____

3. _____
   _____
   _____

INDEX

ABOUT THE AUTHOR

Donna Deeprose is the author of *The Team Coach,* as well as several other books about project management, corporate culture, motivation, and global human resources. She has developed Web-based training, self-study programs, and video scripts. In addition, she has consulted with organizations on teaming, communications, project management, customer service, and other management issues. She recently moved from New York City to a small town along the Hudson River.

MAY 07 LWD